GHOSTS
OF OGDEN,
BRIGHAM CITY
AND LOGAN

JENNIFER JONES

Haunted America

Published by Haunted America
A Division of The History Press
Charleston, SC
www.historypress.net

Copyright © 2017 by Jennifer Jones
All rights reserved

Front cover: Photograph in the Carol M. Highsmith Archive, Library of Congress, Prints and
Photographs Division.
Back cover: Photograph by Panoramio user chetross68; *inset*: photograph by Jennifer Jones.

First published 2017

Manufactured in the United States

ISBN 9781467137850

Library of Congress Control Number: 2017945015

CONTENTS

Foreword, by Helmey Kramer   5
Acknowledgements   7
Introduction   9

PART I. OGDEN AND SURROUNDING AREAS
1. The Haunts of Historic 25th Street   15
2. Twenty-Fifth Street Tunnels   17
3. Electric Alley   20
4. Making Scents Emporium   24
5. Ben Lomond Hotel   29
6. Ogden's Union Station   39
7. Browning Theater   44
8. Spectral Soldiers and Basement Vaults   50
9. The Ghostly Women of the Station   53
10. Killed by the Clock Tower   61
11. Peery's Egyptian Theater   64
12. Rainbow Gardens   68
13. Shooting Star Saloon   71
14. Ogden City Cemetery and Flo's Grave   77
15. The House on Van Buren   81
16. Steed's Pond   84
17. Hobbs Hollow   87

Contents

Part II. Brigham City

18. Crystal Hot Springs   93
19. Brigham City Train Depot   98
20. Bushnell Army Hospital/Indian Schools   101

Part III. Logan and Smithfield

21. The Nunnery   115
22. The Main Theater   118
23. Weeping Woman of Logan City Cemetery   121

Bibliography   125
About the Author   128

FOREWORD

While growing up, one of the greatest lessons for me was the value of questioning the obvious. I soon discovered that most experiences have many layers and that to understand them takes more than a cursory glance. I tend to ponder and research evidence, especially in the field of paranormal phenomena. I am a skeptic.

I've identified three commonalities in places where I've personally experienced ghostly activity. The first is some sort of traumatic event. It could be localized to a specific period or generalized as ongoing and painful. Second is an intensely passionate connection between the living individual(s) at some point and the location itself. The third is desecration of a grave or a burial site. I go into every location with no expectations but remain open to whatever experiences I might encounter. Without documentation of any of the aforementioned circumstances, the chances of documenting supernatural events seem to be reduced significantly, no matter how spooky the place might look.

While preparing to hit the road to film the television show *Haunted Encounters*, my research of one location in Massachusetts was giving me trouble. The prior residents' history, albeit tragic, appeared to be heavily recycled; nothing tied back to the structure itself. Needing another set of eyes, I pointed Jennifer Jones in its direction and got out of her way. What she came up with forced me to change my entire approach to the investigation. I can safely say that the result was incredible and extremely emotional. The overlooked individual from the family was the one still haunting the hallways of the impressive mansion. The matriarch, forced to endure more tragedy than most of us could imagine, followed by dying slowly and painfully, isn't necessarily what makes a good ghost story. But she is without a doubt responsible for this one.

Another recent example is a museum here in Utah that the curator asked us to investigate a few months ago. At first glance, the building's background gave no indication as to why it might be haunted. Jen identified a few key figures that we should focus on. We subsequently identified incredible ghostly interactions and determined that the structure was haunted. We also found out who was haunting it. While recording audio, I asked, "How can we be sure it's you?" The response was a clear and eerie "My name is [omitted to preserve the anonymity of the location]." If we want answers, we must ask the right questions. With Jen in my corner, I have the luxury of always knowing what those questions are.

While the media is often overcrowded with the smoke and mirrors of carnival-like entertainment, there is truth to be found. This is where constantly evolving methodology employed in a scientific dynamic is critical. I truly believe documented history is the most valuable and underused resource in the field of paranormal investigation.

This is important because the dead were once the living. Going on location armed with accurate historical information dramatically increases the chances for spirit interaction. Jennifer's dedication to historical research and documentation is reflected in this book. From haunted spots to urban legends, she tells the stories that were once forgotten or distorted by various imaginations. As you will see in the following pages, Jennifer's writing beautifully marries history with a personal commentary that is a joy to read.

I can say without any doubt that Jennifer Jones is far and away the greatest historian of the haunted that the paranormal community has known. I believe that her unbridled tenacity combined with patience, attention to detail and natural talent give her the ability to find and deliver documented history.

Helmey Kramer

ACKNOWLEDGEMENTS

This book is dedicated to the many souls whose stories I am honored to have researched and been able to share; to my children, who were patient with me over the many hours I spent locked away writing; and finally, to Matthew, without whose help and encouragement this book would have never been written.

INTRODUCTION

G hosts. The topic always seems to draw two distinct reactions: they definitely exist, or there is no such thing! Some of us are drawn to try to learn as much as we can about the paranormal. In the last few years, paranormal TV shows have exploded in popularity. New paranormal teams are popping up every day, as are annual paranormal conferences and ghost walks. What is it about the paranormal world that some people can't seem to get enough of? If they're like me, it's because they're fascinated with the possibility of life existing in some form after we die. Or perhaps they've had their own experiences with something they can't quite explain and they're looking for answers. Whatever their beliefs or backgrounds, it's hard to deny that interest in the paranormal has been around for a very long time. This interest started making front-page news during the spiritualist movement of the Victorian era and steadily gained in popularity with the work of people such as Hans Holzer and Ed and Lorraine Warren. This in turn led to the phenomenon of paranormal TV shows beginning in the late 1990s.

When I was a child, I had an encounter with what I would describe now as a shadow figure. It started me on this path of fascination with ghost stories and tales of haunted places. As an adult, I decided to take my fascination one step further and go out looking for experiences and maybe even some answers. In 2007, I formed a paranormal team and began to investigate reportedly haunted locations. Over the years, I tried to improve the way my team did its work. We tried to investigate locations in such a way as to rule out all natural, explainable causes for things people were reporting.

More times than not we could come up with rational explanations for odd sounds, feelings and other complaints people had. But every now and then, we would encounter things that we couldn't explain away. After doing this for a while, you tend to notice that truly haunted places have a certain feel. To me, the best way to explain it is that it feels as if you're walking into a wall of static electricity. The hairs on my arms and the back of my neck stand up, and I often feel a tingly sensation in my hands and fingers.

In 2012, I was in the process of working toward a degree in history and decided to leave the paranormal team; the pursuit of my degree was a priority, and running a very busy paranormal team took up so much of my time. After leaving the group, I had an idea to combine my love for history and for the paranormal. I began to research the true stories behind haunted locations and urban legends. So many times, stories of haunted locations are passed from person to person, and they begin to change and take on a life of their own. Names and dates get changed, and whatever had occurred was often lost to time. I wanted to know how many of the stories behind these haunted places were based in truth.

What I ended up finding time and again actually surprised me. Maybe it was because I went into this expecting many of the stories to be debunked, only to find that the real history behind the hauntings was so much more fascinating than the stories themselves. Since 2012, I've been blogging about local haunted places and urban legends in the hopes of bringing to light the real stories of the people behind the stories.

When people talk about haunted locations in Utah, they often focus on Salt Lake City, simply because it's Utah's capital city. Salt Lake City has many interesting haunted locations, don't get me wrong. But there are so many great haunted places north of Salt Lake City that people aren't aware of or simply don't get much attention. The northern Wasatch Range has some really haunted places! From Ogden and surrounding areas to Brigham City, Logan and everywhere in between, you'll find remarkable locations with fascinating histories and tales of ghostly encounters.

This book focuses on locations in and around the city of Ogden, in part because it's the biggest city in Utah north of Salt Lake, and also because it happens to have the wildest history of any Utah city. Ogden is one of those unique towns in America that has managed to hold on to its wild past and incorporate that into its present. The city hasn't torn down everything that is old and replaced it with new buildings. It's a great mix of old and new, and you can feel the history this town has to offer as you walk down Twenty-Fifth Street.

Ogden was a railroad and cattle town, being a major hub in the western United States for stock transport. It shouldn't come as a surprise that the Union Station on Twenty-Fifth Street and Wall Avenue is known as one of the most haunted locations in the city. Given the length of the building's history, the sheer number of people who have passed through its doors over the years and a few tragic events, it has all the makings for a haunted building. The same goes for Twenty-Fifth Street, which was once considered to be so wild that respectable people would not be caught anywhere near the short stretch of road that runs from the Union Station east to the Ben Lomond Hotel. The following are stories of some of the most haunted locations in northern Utah along the Wasatch Range based on my experiences and research, as well as the stories of the people who live or work in the locations.

PART I

OGDEN AND SURROUNDING AREAS

1

THE HAUNTS OF HISTORIC 25TH STREET

Having been the center of activity of the city of Ogden for almost 150 years, Historic 25th Street is the place to go for interesting history and spooky tales. Starting in front of the Ben Lomond Hotel on Twenty-Fifth Street and Washington Boulevard, the historic portion of Twenty-Fifth Street runs three blocks west, terminating in front of the Union Station. At one time, Ogden had nine streetcar lines, the most popular running down the heart of the city on Twenty-Fifth, ending in front of the depot. Ogden soon developed a wild reputation, a result of its rapid growth, the large number of travelers coming and going through the city and the fact that the Church of Jesus Christ of Latter-day Saints didn't have as much influence in Ogden as it did in Salt Lake City.

With a history of brothels in the upstairs of a handful of businesses lining Twenty-Fifth Street and Electric Alley, numerous saloons, gambling halls and speakeasies, along with the rumors of bootleg tunnels, it's no wonder this short stretch of road is such a draw to Ogdenites and tourists alike. Today, Twenty-Fifth Street is a wonderful, family-friendly place to go. Almost every weekend, there is some type of event going on, such as a historic car show or a festival. In the summer, the park around the municipal building hosts a fantastic farmer's market; at Christmastime, it's decked out in thousands of lights with a locally sponsored Christmas village that draws visitors from across the state.

You can eat in one of the many unique restaurants that line the street, sitting next to the original exposed handmade brick walls. I often wonder how many people realize they're shopping in a store that was at one time a brothel or eating lunch in a building that was once a saloon where more than one person died in a fight. If those walls could talk, they would have quite the stories to tell!

2
Twenty-Fifth Street Tunnels

It is impossible to properly talk about the history of Twenty-Fifth Street, or Ogden for that matter, without touching on the topic of the tunnels. One of the questions I'm most often asked is, "Have you ever been inside of the tunnels?" Ogden's best-kept secret—or urban legend, depending on whom you talk to—is the presence of tunnels somewhere under Twenty-Fifth Street. While many city officials and local historians have long denied that they ever existed, others are adamant about their existence.

The tunnels are said to have been constructed by Chinese immigrants who stayed in Ogden after completion of the transcontinental railroad. They were often referred to in newspapers as "Celestials" (China was known as the Celestial Empire in the late nineteenth century). These workers had spent many months tunneling through the Sierra Nevada mountain range laying railroad track, so it's not difficult to see how they could dig tunnels under Twenty-Fifth Street. And since they were discriminated against by many in Ogden, it's not a surprise they would use tunnels to move around town, avoiding having to deal with nasty comments and harassment.

The tunnels are said to have been used to move alcohol during Prohibition, functioned as hidden opium dens, hid illegal gambling operations and offered secret entrances to brothels and quick exits from speakeasies. There are even tales of members of organized crime using the tunnels to imprison people who owed them money or had wronged them in some way. Some say that a tunnel ran from the basement of the Ben Lomond Hotel all the way down Twenty-Fifth Street to the basement of the Union Station. Others say the "tunnels" were nothing more than a couple of small, interconnected basements.

Determining the truth behind the Ogden tunnels is made difficult by the fact that I have never been able to find a single mention of the tunnels in any historical publication, searching all the way back to the late 1860s. This could mean they weren't mentioned because they never existed. But it may also be the case that they weren't discussed because they weren't supposed to exist. The latter case makes more sense to me. If they existed and were used for illegal purposes, it's not something that would have been spoken about publicly. But, considering that the days of illegal booze running, speakeasies and brothels are long gone, what would keep people from speaking publicly about them now?

While I have yet to gain access to the tunnels, I have seen what appears to be bricked-up or cemented doorways in more than one basement on Twenty-Fifth Street. All of these old doorways were at the front of the buildings, facing the street. For the longest time, I held the opinion that it was nothing more than a few businesses having interconnected basement areas. These could have been old coal chutes or delivery entrances, which buildings used to have on the sidewalks in front of their stores. It wouldn't be unheard of for those areas to have served as opium dens, gambling rooms or small speakeasies.

My views have changed since doing more in-depth research for this book. I was recently shown around the basement of a business on Twenty-Fifth Street that had what appeared to be two separate sealed doorways. Instead of these being at the south end of the building facing Twenty-Fifth, they were on the east and west sides. Interestingly enough, this location sits directly in front of what was once Electric Alley, the red-light district of Ogden in the early twentieth century. It is also on the corner, so there was no building on the east side for this entrance to connect to. That is, unless this entrance connected to a tunnel that ran under the street. The location of the doorway on the west side of the basement would have pointed to the heart of Electric Alley. It was extremely intriguing to me, to say the least!

Years ago, while talking to the manager of the Union Station, the topic of the tunnels came up in our conversation. She told me how she and a co-worker walked along the perimeter of the dirt-floor basement, looking for any evidence of old doorways or tunnels. They found nothing. While investigating the Union Station, I was able to spend quite a bit of time in the basement, including the dirt crawlspace area, and saw no evidence of doorways. The foundation of the current Union Station is the original stone foundation of the previous building, constructed in 1889. There could not have been an entrance since closed up without it being obvious. So, while I think that there were or are tunnels around Twenty-Fifth Street, I don't believe that there was a tunnel running all the way from the station to the Ben Lomond Hotel. Maybe one day there will be definitive proof of what lies behind all of those bricked-up doorways.

I'm not sure if we will ever know the full extent of the tunnels in Ogden. I believe they definitely existed, and I think that there was at least one or two that were more than just interconnected basements. I've heard stories of work being done on Twenty-Fifth Street in the 1970s when heavy equipment broke through the sidewalk into some of these tunnels. It was then that city officials sealed off and filled in what tunnels remained. This seems like a plausible story to me, but I've been unable to find any trace of this in any newspapers of the time.

3

ELECTRIC ALLEY

If you've ever been to Twenty-Fifth Street on a busy weekend, you know that it can be difficult to find parking on the street. Luckily, Ogden has done a great job of providing free parking around the area. One of the biggest parking lots is located directly behind the shops on lower Twenty-Fifth Street. What brought my attention to this lot is that it has an odd street sign at the entrance: "Electric Alley." The first time I saw it, I remember thinking it was somewhat strange to have a street sign at the entrance to a parking lot. But as I learned more about Ogden's history, I realized that this sign was a direct nod to part of Ogden's naughty past: the red-light district. Shocking, right? Ogden had a red-light district? Even though Electric Alley was razed in the 1950s to clean up the area and eventually make room for a large hotel and parking lot, I think it is directly connected to many of the ghost stories from Twenty-Fifth Street.

Spurred on by the dramatic influx of visitors to Ogden following construction of the train depot, Electric Alley came into existence sometime in the late 1880s. By the late 1890s, Ogden had a flourishing red-light district that operated out in the open. Electric Alley ran east to west, from Grant to Lincoln Avenues between Twenty-Fourth and Twenty-Fifth Streets. It was mostly hidden from view by the buildings fronting Twenty-Fourth and Twenty-Fifth, and that's exactly how people wanted it to be. During that time, you could walk down the north side of Twenty-Fifth Street toward the Union Station and slip quickly into a narrow, dark walkway between the Davenport Saloon and the London Ice Cream Parlor. Entering this walkway

Entrance to former site of Electric Alley, Ogden, Utah. *Photograph by Jennifer Jones.*

would take you directly into the heart of Electric Alley. The Davenport Saloon is now a hair salon, and the London Ice Cream Parlor is home to a restaurant. Little else about this shortcut has changed.

Entering Electric Alley, one was greeted by a row of small, eight-by-eight-foot brick houses, or "cribs," as they were known. There was also a large house, described in 1910 by the Ogden Betterment League as a "great pretentious building." This house belonged to Utah's most famous

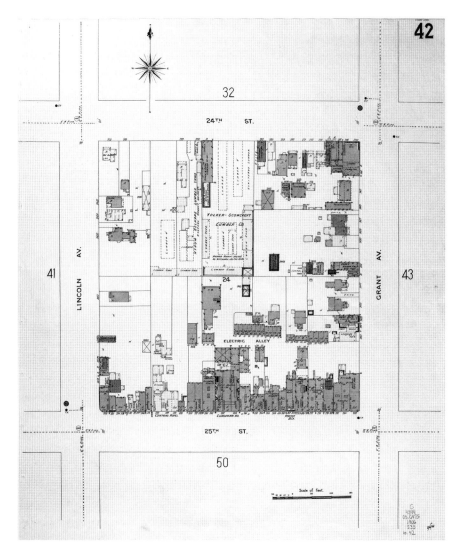

Map of Electric Alley, Ogden, Utah. *Sheet 42, 1906 Sanborn Fire Map, J. Willard Marriot Library, University of Utah.*

madam, a woman who was more or less in charge of Electric Alley, Dora Belle Topham. Topham was more well known by her alias, Belle London. Not only was Belle London a well-known madam, she was also a shrewd businesswoman who owned more property on Twenty-Fifth Street at the end of the nineteenth century than almost anyone else in town. Despite her choice of profession, she was respected by city officials and business leaders.

Modern view of Electric Alley site, view of entrance walkway, Ogden, Utah. *Photograph by Jennifer Jones.*

The interesting thing about Electric Alley is that not only were city officials completely aware of what went on there, but they also used it as a way to increase revenue. Each woman working in one of the cribs or brothels paid Belle London rent of $2 a day or $12 a week (today, $52 a day or $315 a week). City officials would make the rounds through Electric Alley on the twentieth of each month to collect "fines." Belle London was fined $15 a month, and each woman working out of one of the cribs was fined $5. It's no wonder why the city turned a blind eye to Electric Alley—it was making a lot of money. Along with increased revenue came an increase in violent crimes. While conducting research for this book, I came across more than one article detailing incidents of men beating or killing each other, fighting over the same woman in one of the brothels.

Belle London and the city maintained this understanding until 1912, when immense pressure from civic leagues forced city officials to shut down Ogden's red-light district. After thirty years, the women of Electric Alley were said to have been run out of town. By 1913, the cribs of Electric Alley were being converted into cold-storage units for use by local businesses and probably the Union Station as well. While the city may have made it look like it was cleaning up Twenty-Fifth Street, in reality, many of the women just moved into hidden brothels in the hotels and second-floor rooming houses lining the street. According to many business owners on this street, many of the women have remained, even after death.

4

MAKING SCENTS EMPORIUM

Making Scents Emporium is a little shop located on the first floor of an original Twenty-Fifth Street building at Grant Avenue. Erected in 1895, the building has served as a restaurant, saloon, hotel, rooming house, bus depot and even apartments. It now houses a few different businesses and office space and has been a hotbed of paranormal activity for quite some time. It also happens to sit directly in front of what was once a main entrance to Electric Alley.

Because the older buildings have held various types of businesses through the years, it makes the stories of paranormal activity much more interesting. Many of the business owners I have talked to describe seeing apparitions that appear to be from different periods, wearing clothing from the late 1800s, for example, or the 1920s or '30s. This is the case with Making Scents Emporium, according to the store's owner, Larry Baird.

I recently sat down with Larry to talk about the ghostly encounters he's experienced while working in the store. He said that when he and his friends first moved into the store, they did not believe in ghosts, but his beliefs quickly changed. He said he noticed odd things happening in the building almost as soon as he moved in and began to refurbish and remodel the store. I wasn't surprised when he told me that activity began happening as they were making changes to the building. Remodeling a location often spurs paranormal activity or causes the activity to increase.

One of the first things he experienced took place while he was giving a tour of his basement to a group of people who had stopped by the store while on a walking ghost tour of Ogden. He left half of the group downstairs and came back to the first floor with the rest of the group. While waiting for the group to finish looking around his shop, he saw a man in his peripheral vision wearing a dark-colored, old-fashioned suit walk toward him so close that he brushed his arm as he walked past. He said he instantly felt a chill as the man passed, and he thought to himself how strange it was. Larry then watched as this man disappeared while walking directly through the wall.

West tunnel entrance under Making Scents, Twenty-Fifth Street, Ogden, Utah. *Photograph by Jennifer Jones.*

Most of the paranormal activity Larry has encountered here occurred in the basement. It's a large basement that stretches the length of the store. The walls are made of stone, and the original large wooden beams that support the first floor are exposed. While working in the basement one day cleaning and organizing his stock, Larry made a curious discovery. Tucked under one of the heavy beams was an old braided lock of light-brown hair. I later made a discovery that made Larry's find even more interesting. In the back of the basement are two sealed doorways, one on the west side of the room and the other directly across from it on the east side. The doorway on the west side of the room, if it led to a passage that went to the ground level, would have opened onto Electric Alley. This building was owned by Belle London from 1903 until 1911. Could the braid have come from one of the ladies who worked in Electric Alley? Why would someone hide a braid of hair under basement floorboards? Larry has also found old whiskey bottles and pieces of old wallpaper hidden in nooks and crannies in the basement.

Larry and other people who have spent time in the store when the shop is closed have also reported the sound of boots on a wood floor. The store originally had wood floors on the main level, which was covered by cement floors years ago while the building was being refurbished. A few days after hearing that, they found dusty boot prints

East tunnel entrance under Making Scents leading to the federal courthouse, Twenty-Fifth Street, Ogden, Utah. *Photograph by Jennifer Jones.*

on a piece of old carpet in the basement. The prints led to a wall, as if something or someone had walked through the wall. Psychics who have visited the store have said there is a young female spirit that spends a lot of time in the store, as well as a man whom they refer to as the "Captain." He is said to have been an Ogden police officer in the early 1900s and was responsible for visiting the various brothels to collect the fines from the working girls.

While looking into the history of the building, I found that it housed the St. Louis Saloon in the early 1900s and was a frequent destination for the Ogden police. Numerous raids were conducted, mainly looking for illegal gambling operations. It seems as if the St. Louis Saloon was a pretty wild place in the early 1900s. The *Ogden Standard Examiner* reported in September 1906 that a waiter jumped out of the second-floor window, landing headfirst on the sidewalk below and miraculously surviving.

One of the most startling occurrences at Making Scents happened when some people came to the store and asked Larry if he would show them the bricked-up tunnel entrances in the basement. It was almost closing time, so Larry said if they could wait a few minutes he would take them downstairs once he closed up shop. He locked the front door and went to take the group into the basement, only to find that the basement door wouldn't open. Something was pushed up against it from the other side. There is only one entrance to the basement, and Larry couldn't understand how the door could be blocked—to get out of the basement one would have had to come through that door, and he was the only one in the store that night. He told me it was the strangest thing—he had been down in the basement earlier that evening, and there was nothing close to the door that could have fallen over and blocked it. He was able to push the door open enough to squeeze through. He found that some supplies he kept in the basement had been stacked up against the door. Somewhat rattled, he laughed it off and led the people into the basement to have a look around.

It wouldn't be the last strange thing to happen in the basement. Larry often let paranormal teams come in after closing to investigate the building. For groups he knew well and trusted, he allowed them to lock up the building when they were done so he wouldn't have to hang out all night. One morning following an investigation, he came into the shop and went into the basement to get some supplies. He saw broken glass all over the floor. A few jars he used for his soaps and lotions, previously stacked on shelves, lay shattered in the middle of the room.

Larry immediately called the person in charge of the group to complain. He told me that he was shocked, because he had known this group for some time, had never had any problems with them in the past and didn't think they would damage something without at least leaving a note or cleaning it up. When he asked the director of the team what had happened the night before and why the basement was such a mess, the man told Larry they had left the store in the condition they found it. Larry told me that the man was extremely apologetic and sounded legitimately surprised. Larry believes that whatever broke the jars did it after the team had left for the night and was possibly upset because the paranormal team had been trying to provoke the spirits during its investigation.

Other paranormal teams have captured some very clear electronic voice phenomenon (EVP) recordings in the shop, mainly in the basement. Usually, it is the sound of a man's voice that is caught during investigations.

I wasn't able to find any proof that a young girl died on the premises, but there were quite a few deaths at this location. Most of the deaths occurred from the late 1920s to the 1950s and happened in the upstairs portion of the building when it was the Community Hotel. All deaths were attributed to natural causes, such as old age. A couple of deaths occurred in the saloon itself. One man, George Jefferson, dropped dead in the St. Louis Saloon, according to the *Salt Lake Telegram* of September 25, 1905. He was referred to as a "giant of a man" who was unfamiliar to those who frequented the saloon. It was later found that George Jefferson was a sailor in the U.S. Navy who had recently been honorably discharged and was passing through Ogden on his way to visit family in Wisconsin. Officials were unable to locate any relatives to claim his body, and he was buried with military honors in Ogden City Cemetery.

Those who seem to remain at this store and make themselves known from time to time don't bother Larry at all. He says he's never felt threatened or scared; he has come to accept the strange activity as a quirk of the building. He says his outlook on the paranormal has changed completely since working in the store. He's not sure how to explain any of it, but he definitely feels like there are spirits of the past still hanging around his store.

5

BEN LOMOND HOTEL

The Ben Lomond Hotel, located on the corner of Washington Boulevard and Twenty-Fifth Street, is rumored to be one of the most haunted places in Ogden. As with other locations I've researched, the truth behind the Ben Lomond's past was far more interesting and tragic than I was expecting. Before starting my research, I tried to find as many stories about the hotel's ghosts as I could, to see if any of these stories had some truth to them.

The most popular tale involves a bride who came to the hotel on her honeymoon and tragically drowned in the bathtub of room 1102. Shortly after her death, it's said that her son arrived at the hotel to gather her personal belongings. He was so distraught over her death that he committed suicide in the adjoining room, room 1101. Oddly enough, no mention is ever made of her groom.

It seems the eleventh floor is the focus of most of the stories. In addition to the bride, it's also said that a woman came to live at the Ben Lomond during World War II to await her son's return from service. The story goes on to say that she died in room 1102 or 1106, either passing from natural causes without knowing that her son was already dead or hearing of her son's death and dying from a broken heart. Other rumors about who may be haunting the hotel involve a Mrs. Eccles, wife of a former owner, as well as a hotel clerk who was murdered in the lobby.

Hotel staff have said that they receive many calls from people staying at the hotel complaining of odd noises coming from the room next to them. When the staff goes to investigate, they find that the room where the noises

Ben Lomond Suites Historic Hotel in Ogden, Utah. Built in 1927, it is an example of Italian Renaissance Revival style in Utah. *Photo by Wikicommons user Ricardo630 (CC BY-SA 3.0).*

are said to be coming from are empty. Housekeepers have complained of putting objects on a table while cleaning a room, only to turn around and find the same object in the middle of the bed. There have been reports of the scent of old-fashioned lavender perfume and, believe it or not, ghost cats. The elevators also seem to be a hot spot for weird experiences and have a mind of their own. Night staff report the elevator doors opening at the lobby, then closing, and the elevator going to various floors, only to return to the lobby and the doors opening again.

I have stayed at the hotel and had my own unusual experience with the elevator. My daughter and I were in the lobby waiting for the elevator to take us to the sixth floor, where our room was. We got in the elevator and were the only guests in the elevator at the time. I pressed the button for the sixth floor, the button lit up, the doors closed and the elevator began to ascend. We got to the sixth floor, but the elevator kept going. It then stopped at the tenth floor. The doors opened. I really expected to see someone standing there waiting for the elevator, but no one was there. The hallway was completely empty. Knowing the history of the hotel, I stepped out into the hallway and was surprised not only to see no one in the area, but

Lobby of the Ben Lomond Hotel. *Photograph by Jennifer Jones.*

also that it seemed to be quiet—too quiet. It sounds weird, but after you've been investigating the paranormal for a few years, you become familiar with the lack of expected noise. There were no housekeeping carts, no sounds coming from the rooms on that floor—it was completely still. I got back into the elevator and again pressed the button for the sixth floor. We continued on our way. Could it have been just a weird mechanical issue? Most definitely, I thought. It's an old elevator. But after doing more research on the hotel's history, I am not so sure.

The Ben Lomond is considered one of Utah's three grand hotels, and it's the only one of those three still operating as a hotel. While Ogden has always had numerous hotels near Twenty-Fifth Street, this was the hotel to choose if you had money. This is where notable people passing through Ogden stayed, such as John Wayne, Louis Armstrong and even Al Capone.

Since the current building's construction in 1927, it has held the title of the largest hotel in Ogden, and for many years it was also the tallest building in the city, at fourteen floors. Although a hotel has stood on this corner since July 1891, the Ben Lomond is not the original hotel. That status belongs to the Reed Hotel (1891–1926). The Reed was six stories tall, had 140 rooms, as well as a restaurant on the fifth floor that gave diners a great view of Mount Ben Lomond in the distance.

The Reed Hotel recorded its first death three days before the hotel's grand opening, on June 30, 1891. William B. Steele was found dead in bed around 10:00 p.m., finally succumbing to the effects of tuberculosis. Steele, the brother-in-law of one of the hotel's proprietors, had recently moved to Utah, believing the dry air would help improve his condition. Maybe this was a foreshadowing of things to come, because from 1891 until the Reed was remodeled into the Bigelow Hotel, eight more deaths occurred on the property.

Most of the recorded deaths I came across during my research were due to old age or other natural causes. However, there were a few that were incredibly tragic. The first was a suicide that occurred on September 8, 1902. A married couple by the name of Mr. and Mrs. Van Alen had recently moved into one of the hotel's apartments, occupying two rooms on the third floor of the Reed Hotel facing Twenty-Fifth Street. William Van Alen was a prominent businessman from California. Newspaper reports stated that the couple had been married for a few years, and there were rumors that it wasn't exactly a happy marriage. Tide Helen Van Alen had been suffering from "nervousness and insomnia," according to her friends and family. Mr. Van Alen left the apartment for work that morning and later told detectives he reminded his wife to make an appointment with her physician for further treatment. When he came back to the hotel around noon, he found their apartment door locked. There was no response when he knocked on the door repeatedly. He had to fetch the bellboy from the lobby to help him open the door. Once inside, they found Mrs. Van Alen deceased in the bed with a gun in her hand. In her other hand she clutched a small Bible with

Right: Ben Lomond Hotel elevators. Paranormal activity is often reported in this area of the hotel. *Photograph by Jennifer Jones.*

Below: Reed Hotel. *American Hotel Association of the United States and Canada American Hotel Association, New York, Official Hotel Red Book and Directory Company.*

Hot and Cold Water and Telephones in all Rooms

Two Elevators   Three Fire Escapes

A Quarter of a Million Investment

THE REED
OGDEN, UTAH

The Leading Hotel of the City

Commercial Men's Headquarters
Thirty well-equipped Sample Rooms
First-class Cafe in Connection

European Plan

RATES : (use public bath) $1.00 to $1.50 per day
RATES : (with private bath) $1.50 to $2.50 per day

FREE AUTO-BUS TO AND FROM ALL TRAINS

H. C. BIGELOW, Prop.

a letter inside. Mrs. Van Alen had shot herself in the head. The letter was found to be her last will and testament, which she had apparently written that morning. Mrs. Van Alen was only thirty-eight years old.

The first accidental death came a few years before the Reed Hotel was partially demolished and remodeled into the Ben Lomond. On September 26, 1921, a forty-eight-year-old cook named Asugi "Harry" Nakano fell three stories down the freight elevator shaft to his death. A fairly new employee of the hotel, he was working as a cook for one of the hotel's cafés. At approximately 11:30 that morning, he had a handful of dishes or other kitchen supplies and headed to the freight elevator. No one witnessed the accident, so it's not certain if he just wasn't paying attention or couldn't see through what he was carrying, but he stepped into the elevator shaft not realizing there was no elevator waiting for him at that floor. Other employees heard his fall and rushed to his aid. But there was nothing they could do to help him, and he died a short time later. He is buried in the Japanese section of Ogden City Cemetery.

In 1926, after thirty-five years in business, the Reed Hotel was partially demolished, and the new Bigelow Hotel emerged. The first four floors of the Reed Hotel remained, and additional floors were added. The Bigelow Hotel opened on June 3, 1927, boasting 350 guest rooms, each with a private bath. There were also eleven dining rooms, including a coffee shop. Each dining room had its own theme, including an Arabian-styled coffee shop, a Florentine palace ballroom, an Old Spanish business meeting room, two English rooms and a Japanese tearoom. When it opened, it was by far the most luxurious hotel Ogden had ever seen. It was a great place for travelers to relax after getting off the train at the Union Station.

Unfortunately, it didn't take long for the next death to occur. This time, it was murder. On March 9, 1929, the Utah Canners Association hosted its annual convention at the Bigelow Hotel. An attendee of the convention, Dan Rowland, invited a few friends up to his room, room 1228, for a few drinks. The plan was to have some quick drinks and then head back to the ballroom for more dancing. As this was 1929, Prohibition was in full effect, and alcoholic drinks would not have been available at the hotel. Another man, Edward Spelman, had somehow attached himself to this group of people and followed them upstairs, even though he didn't know any of them. While in the room, the wife of one of Dan's friends had too much to drink and decided to stay in the room and lie down for a while as the rest of the group went downstairs to dance. Spelman left with the others and then, at some point, came back to the room. Dan Rowland's date realized she left her hat in his room, and she and Dan returned to room 1228 to grab it. When they walked in, they found Edward Spelman "attacking" the unconscious woman lying on the bed.

Rowland immediately confronted Spelman and would later tell detectives that he was trying to get Spelman down into the lobby of the hotel so that he could notify hotel staff and the police what had happened. Not surprisingly, Spelman did not like this idea and, according to witnesses, was arguing with Rowland while walking toward the elevator. Spelman raised his hand to strike Rowland and missed. Rowland immediately swung back, hitting Spelman square on the chin. Spelman went down, hitting his head on the wall, killing him instantly.

When detectives arrived, they found Edward Spelman lying dead in front of room 1219. They carried his body into room 1215, as it was vacant at the time. At the autopsy, it was discovered that he died from a ruptured artery. Dan Rowland was later charged and acquitted of Spelman's murder. He was, however, found guilty of illegal possession of liquor and fined $150.

A few years after the death of Edward Spelman, the hotel was purchased by Marriner S. Eccles and its name changed to Hotel Ben Lomond in 1933. For a few years, everything was quiet at the hotel and business was great. That changed in 1939, with one of the oddest stories I've come across while researching haunted places. On the afternoon of Monday, January 23, 1939, Glen Jackson, twenty-nine, and Elmo Chapman, thirty-two, got out of a taxi in front of the hotel on Washington Boulevard. They pushed past a bellboy standing at the doors of the hotel and managed to get into an elevator operated by a young woman. They asked her to take them to the top floor, but after initially agreeing to do so, she felt something was off and took them back to the lobby. She would later tell investigators that she had a feeling something wasn't right about the pair and wanted to find someone in the lobby who could help her.

When she was unable to find anyone to help her, she closed the elevator door and started up again, letting the two men out on the thirteenth floor. The men made their way to the window at the end of the hallway on the south side of the building. Finding the window unlocked, Glen Jackson leapt out of the window, followed shortly thereafter by Elmo Chapman. An investigation was performed by Ogden detectives; it is believed the two were despondent after having recently lost their jobs. Glen Jackson is buried in Ogden City

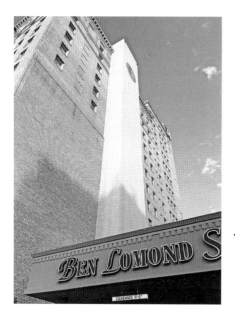

Ben Lomond Hotel, Ogden, Utah. *Photograph by Jennifer Jones.*

Cemetery; Elmo Chapman is buried nearby in Aultorest Cemetery.

In the years following, there were some natural deaths and at least one more suicide at the hotel. As rail travel declined, Ogden tourism began to decline and the local area began to change. In October 1976, one of the most senseless and brutal murders in Ogden took place at the Hotel Ben Lomond. Henry Topping Jr., sixty-five, worked at the hotel as a desk clerk. In the early morning of Sunday, October 24, Henry was going about his nightly tasks, which that evening included catching water from a leaking fountain in the hotel lobby. While carrying buckets of water, he was attacked from behind and stabbed to death. His body was found shortly before 2:00 a.m. on the floor in the middle of the lobby. The attacker stole his wallet and $370 from the hotel's cash register and disappeared into the dark streets of Ogden. Topping was described as one of the nicest people one could meet. Those who knew him said he would have given his attacker the money if given the chance. The police eventually captured a fifteen-year-old boy, who was charged and convicted for his murder.

Not all of the ghosts that may haunt the hotel remain here due to tragedy. Through the years, the hotel also had a number of fully furnished apartments that were available for lease. For many years, May Eccles, the former wife of Marriner Eccles, lived in one of the apartments on the eleventh floor. She was said to have loved the hotel, often hosting lavish parties there. In the last years of her life, she was bedridden in her apartment. The staff knew she was there, but she was very rarely seen. May Eccles died in a local hospital in 1964 at the age of seventy. Staff who knew her believed that she was one of the spirits who lingered at the hotel after her death. Housekeepers and guests alike report the scent of old-fashioned lavender perfume that Mrs. Eccles was quite fond of. Of all the reports of ghostly activity, the most popular is that of the apparition of an

Fountain in the lobby of the Ben Lomond Hotel, probable site of the murder of Henry Topping Jr. *Photograph by Jennifer Jones.*

older lady. She has been spotted throughout the hotel, but most sightings are reported on the eleventh floor.

If the reports of an elevator with a mind of its own, the scent of old-fashioned perfume, phantom phone calls from empty rooms, strange sounds and things being moved around the rooms isn't enough, this hotel has ghost cats. Reports of ghost cats aren't too unusual in the paranormal field, although I haven't come across many that haunt a hotel. Guests and staff alike have reported seeing a cat that promptly disappears into thin air. It is most often seen on the eleventh floor.

Like other haunted places, the Hotel Ben Lomond has seen enough tragedy that it's not hard to believe it may be haunted. The hotel could be home to restless spirits that feel as though they have unfinished business, or those that had a distinct connection to the location, such as Mrs. Eccles—possibly even her cat.

6

OGDEN'S UNION STATION

It's practically impossible to miss the Union Station when visiting downtown Ogden. Located on Wall Avenue at the end of Historic 25th Street, it stands large and important, harkening back to a different era. At night, the Union Station's large neon sign on the roof lights up the lower end of Twenty-Fifth Street in red, drawing attention to the building. Sometimes when I'm on Twenty-Fifth Street with family or friends and I see the Union Station all lit up, it makes me wonder what it must have been like when it was still used as a train depot and it was full of people in a hurry to get to various destinations. I can imagine that the entire area was bustling with cars, people and trucks carrying freight to the depot in order to make the next train. If you cast your mind even further back in time, the area would have been busy with people walking, on horseback and riding in horse-drawn carriages. I imagine that it was not only busy and crowded, but it would also have been loud with the sounds of people, horses, trains and numerous bells and whistles.

To give you an idea of how important the Union Station was not only for the city of Ogden but also for rail travel in the United States, every train headed to the West Coast from the East Coast or vice versa had to stop at Ogden's depot to transfer passengers from the Union Pacific line to the Central Pacific line. Imagine one of the busiest airports in the United States today—that would be the closest modern equivalent to Ogden's Union Station at the height of rail travel. And it wasn't just passenger travel. The station dealt with all types of freight, including cattle, and at the height of

Left: Ogden, Utah, Union Station, summer of 1976. *Photograph by Bruce Fingerhood (CC BY 2.0).*

Below: A view of the track side of the Ogden Union Station from the Twelfth Street viaduct, with the FrontRunner tracks on the right. *Photo by Wikicommons user an Errant Knight (CC BY-SA 4.0).*

World War II, it saw thousands of military men off to war and welcomed back just as many before sending them to their hometown or to nearby Bushnell Army Hospital for rehabilitation and treatment.

Ogden has had a train depot in the area since 1869, and in that exact spot since 1889. The town as it exists today has pretty much grown up around the depot. While many of the nearby factories, warehouses and other buildings that existed simply due to the Union Station have been torn down, quite a few still exist, and most are just down the street from the station. It's part of why I love living in Ogden. It's a city that didn't feel the need to destroy the old to make way for the new. It has found a way to incorporate the new with the old, maintaining the city's great and fascinating history—and the ghosts.

The Union Station today is home to four museums, a gift shop, a restaurant and numerous offices. While the museums have replaced the baggage area, some of the train platforms and other areas of the station, it is easy to imagine what the station looked like when hundreds of people were passing through its doors every day. Shortly after the completion of the transcontinental railroad in March 1869, it was decided that Ogden would be the main intercontinental hub, or junction city. A small, two-story depot was built in November 1869 a short distance from where the current Union Station stands today. This depot was built closer to the Weber River, and people had to walk along a quarter-mile length of boardwalk through swampy marshes to get to the shops and hotels. While it was practically too small from the start, it managed to survive for twenty years despite ongoing complaints from citizens and city officials.

On July 31, 1889, a new depot constructed out of red brick in the popular Romanesque style was opened to the public. The most noticeable feature of this building was a large clock tower located above the middle of the station. This now infamous clock tower may have played a role in at least one of the station's most famous ghost stories. The depot also held thirty-three hotel rooms, a barbershop, separate waiting areas for men and women and a restaurant to serve the needs of travelers passing through Ogden. However, the Victorian-era depot only survived for thirty-four years before disaster struck.

In 1923, a fire destroyed a good portion of the station; instead of repairing the damage, Union Pacific gave in to public outcry and built a new depot directly on the old stone foundation of the previous building. Completed in 1924, it boasted a very large, open lobby with fifty-six-foot-high ceilings, a lunch counter and newsstand for busy travelers, as well as a small emergency hospital. The second-floor hotel that existed in the previous building was gone, replaced by Southern Pacific Railroad and the Ogden Union Railway & Depot Company offices on one end and the Union Pacific Telegraph Department offices on the other.

Rail travel continued to grow in popularity. By 1944, during peak war traffic, as many as 120 trains per day passed through the depot. Passenger trains accounted for approximately half of all trains that stopped at the Union Station, with mail, livestock and various freight making up the rest.

Union Station, Ogden, Utah. *Photograph by Jennifer Jones.*

After the war, passenger rail travel began to slowly decline; by 1972, only one train a day stopped at the depot. In 1977, after 108 years of Ogden having a train depot, the station was closed, and Union Pacific subsequently leased it to the City of Ogden for use as a museum.

Over the years, reports of paranormal activity at the Union Station began circulating among museum staff and visitors until it became well known in the area that the station was one of the most haunted locations not only in Ogden but also throughout the state of Utah. Paranormal activity that has been reported over the years include shadow figures and full-bodied apparitions, disembodied voices, lights turning on and off and the elevator moving on its own. When I moved to Utah and created a paranormal team to investigate haunted places, the Union Station was the one site I could not wait to explore. It quickly became my favorite haunted spot in Ogden.

Through the years, I've been able to investigate the Union Station many times, and it seems to be one of those haunted locations that is either really active or totally dead (pun intended). There are a few areas of the station that are known to be more active than others. I feel that the hot spots of the station are the Browning Theater and theater annex, the long hallway connected to the Myra Powell Gallery and the John M. Browning Firearms Museum. Other people might have a different opinion about what parts of the station are the most haunted, but these areas are where I have experienced activity during the years I was actively investigating the paranormal. After investigating the station so many times, I wanted to know if any of the popular stories surrounding the Union Station's ghosts could be backed by historical fact? When I began researching things that occurred at the Union Station in the last 127 years, I was shocked with some of the events that took place in this building.

7

BROWNING THEATER

During one investigation, I was with a friend of mine in what is now known as the Browning Theater, and we began to get unusual spikes on our EMF meters. An EMF meter detects fields created by electrically charged moving objects. One of the theories about the paranormal is that ghosts use, for lack of a better term, electromagnetic energy to materialize. During an investigation, if we noticed a sudden increase in our EMF meter, we would usually stop and spend a little more time in that area.

The Browning Theater is a very large, open room with the main entrances at the south end of the building and a large stage at the north end. The wall that faces the train tracks has a few large windows that at one time looked directly onto the train platform. Today, that area is enclosed and is referred to as the theater annex. We walked farther into the theater and headed toward the stage, where people have reported activity, mainly seeing shadowy figures and hearing voices and footsteps. We stood near the stage for a few minutes acclimating ourselves to the natural sounds of the room, such as the A/C system, noises from outside and the sounds an old building makes when settling. To our left was a door that opened to the theater annex; it was propped open.

We thought we heard footsteps in the annex, so we headed in that direction to see if another member of the team was in that area or possibly outside of the building, walking along the train tracks. When I got farther into the annex, it was as if the area had an electrical charge, like I had stepped through a wall of static electricity. The hairs on my arms and on the back of my neck stood on end, so I immediately stopped and just stood there. I looked up from my EMF meter and saw what appeared to be a shadow figure. It was shaped like a man, about six feet tall, and it moved away from us very quickly toward the south wall and disappeared into the darkness. Robert, a member of our team, and I immediately took off after it, but by the time we got to the end of the annex, there was nothing there. The former train platform was dark and silent, leaving no evidence of what we might have just seen and heard.

One of the best stories of ghostly activity in the Browning Theater comes from the Union Station's longtime handyman, Jarred Whitaker. Jarred was charged with securing the building each night after all other employees and volunteers had left. He's also the one who stayed with the various paranormal teams that have been given permission to investigate the building, and I've enjoyed listening to his many creepy tales over the years. When I asked Jarred to tell me the spookiest thing he's experienced at the station, he immediately said it happened to him one night after he had locked the building up and was headed home. Jarred told me it was a little after 10:30 p.m. and he was about halfway home when he received a phone call from the alarm company, letting him know that an alarm for the lobby door had gone off and someone was apparently walking around the lobby.

He turned his car around and headed back to the station, only to find that no doors were open or unlocked, there were no signs of forced entry and he couldn't see anyone inside the lobby. He got back into his car and again headed for home, making it to about the same point he was before when he got another call from the security company that the same lobby door alarm had gone off again. This time he thought he'd better check it out more thoroughly—someone must be inside the building. He stopped to pick up his dad, and they returned to the station to clear the building together.

When Jarred and his dad got back to the station, they started on the second floor, checking the hallways and rooms to make sure no one had gotten in and was hiding. After they cleared the upstairs, Jarred's dad went outside to walk the perimeter of the building and make sure no doors had been forced open and no windows were smashed. Jarred went to the main floor to set the alarm. As he was getting ready to enter his code, he said he heard a door shut on the north side of the building, in the direction of the Browning Theater. His dad was waiting for him just outside the door closest to the alarm keypad, and Jarred motioned for his dad to come inside. They headed toward the Browning Theater. He said that, as they stood just

A view of the breezeway next to the Browning Theater, Union Station, Ogden. *Photo by Jennifer Jones.*

outside the theater, they both heard what sounded like a couple of people running inside the theater. Jarred immediately ran into the theater, and his dad ran outside and headed toward the back exit just in case they exited the building from the area behind the stage. Jarred said that when he got into the theater it was completely silent. He met his dad at the back door and realized that there was no way anyone who had been in the building could have gotten out without being seen.

Jarred said they headed for home, and just as they pulled into the driveway, his phone rang again. It was the alarm company calling to let him know that the lobby door alarm was going off again. He said he knew it was just the ghosts of the building acting up; he told the alarm company to disregard any further alarms that night. The experiences that both Jarred and I have had in the Browning Theater and annex have been experienced by numerous other people, to the point where this particular ghost is nicknamed Hootie. None of the people I've talked to through the years has ever been able to tell me where this nickname originated. I thought I would do some research and see what I could find. I wanted to know what was different about the Browning Theater and the theater annex that could cause them to be haunted. I began to dig into the history of this part of the building to try to figure out why, of all places, this would be a hotbed of paranormal activity.

When the Union Station was in use as a train depot, this building was not directly connected to the station as it is today. It was a separate building and functioned as a United States Postal Service mail terminal annex. From 1922 until the early 1970s, the Union Station had a railway post office, and this building was used to sort and inspect mail brought by train. But there's actually more to it than that. This building has a history that lends itself to paranormal activity, and it involves a deadly train accident.

On Sunday, December 31, 1944, approximately seventeen miles west of Ogden, one of the deadliest train wrecks in Utah occurred. This train wreck is often referred to as the Bagley Train Wreck, as it occurred near a section of train siding known as Bagley. The Pacific Limited left Chicago on Friday headed to San Francisco. Normally, the Pacific Limited would be one long section, but occasionally, the train was split into two sections. On this day, it comprised two sections, with eighteen passenger cars making up the first section and the mail express train comprising twenty cars. The Pacific Limited had just begun to cross the Great Salt Lake and was in an area known as the Lucin Cutoff.

The Lucin Cutoff was a 102-mile railroad line running from Ogden on the east side of the lake to Lucin, a small railroad community on the west side of the lake. Twelves miles of this line were on a railroad trestle that crossed the water. Earlier that morning, a long and heavy freight train began to have problems while traveling west from Ogden across the Lucin Cutoff. Because of this, the passenger section of the Pacific Limited had to stop and then proceed slowly with caution. For whatever reason, the second section of the Pacific Limited was unaware of the problems and continued to travel at full speed. At 5:14 a.m., in heavy fog, the mail express train plowed into the last passenger car on the first section. In a matter of seconds, train cars telescoped into each other; several cars fell into the cold water of the Great Salt Lake. Wreckage was stretched out over half a mile. By the time the carnage had come to an end, fifty people were killed and eighty-one injured. Of those killed, thirty-five were army and navy soldiers headed home after serving in World War II.

Because the wreck occurred on the Lucin Cutoff, which is surrounded by marshland, the only way help could reach the accident site was by rail. Three trains were sent from Ogden to carry the injured and dead back to the city for medical treatment. The mail terminal annex, now the Browning Theater, was used as a staging point for the injured and a temporary morgue for the dead. The injured were moved to local hospitals, with many of the servicemen being transported to Bushnell Army Hospital in Brigham City. The dead were moved to various local mortuaries until the families could be notified.

It is interesting to note that the disembodied voices of children are often reported in the Browning Theater, captured by EVPs. Among those killed in the Bagley accident was an entire family. The Porter family had been celebrating the holidays with relatives in Utah and were returning home to Nevada when the accident occurred. The entire family perished, including two young girls, Peggy, fourteen, and Mary Frances, eight.

The Bagley train wreck wasn't the only tragedy the Browning Theater has witnessed. A 1938 death was recorded in the northern part of the theater. On the evening of May 29, Amos Allred, a truck loader at the railway mail terminal, arrived at work to start his night shift. He passed through the large, open mailroom and headed toward the employee locker rooms. As he passed through the mailroom he greeted several of his co-workers and appeared to be in good spirits. Several minutes later, a shot was heard coming from the locker room. When workers rushed in, they found Amos lying on the ground, dead, with a gun next to his right hand.

The coroner initially declared the cause of death as suicide, but it was later changed to accidental self-inflicted gunshot. The gun belonged to one of Amos Allred's co-workers. Since he was alone in the locker room, no one is sure why he picked up the gun.

Could the sounds of ghostly children and the ghost referred to as Hootie be shadows of the aftermath of the terrible accident in 1944? Perhaps it's Amos Allred lingering at the scene of his untimely death. It is impossible to say, but the history of this building certainly could explain why so many instances of paranormal activity are reported here.

8

SPECTRAL SOLDIERS
AND BASEMENT VAULTS

On the second floor of the Union Station is the John M. Browning Firearms Museum. John Browning, one of the most well-known firearms designers in the world, was born in Ogden and lived here for most of his life. Almost all of his designs were developed in his Ogden workshop, a replica of which is housed in the Browning Firearms Museum. The museum includes some of John Browning's original design models and many prototypes. There are numerous pistols, rifles, shotguns and machine guns on display. This museum also happens to be another hotspot of paranormal activity. Incidentally, it is next to the long hallway in which many people have reported the scent of old-fashioned perfume and the sight of apparitions.

During my first investigation at the Union Station, I was able to spend some time in the Browning museum, which usually isn't open to paranormal teams. While I didn't experience anything unusual there at the time, later, while reviewing audio I had recorded, I found that I had captured a clear EVP of a man's voice saying "Hello." Even though it was definitely not one of the best EVPs I've gotten at the Union Station, it was interesting because of the activity that is often reported in this area.

Volunteers are stationed throughout the Union Station, and one of them is located at the entrance to the firearms museum. Over the years, both volunteers and visitors of the firearms museum have reported seeing two different men wearing old-fashioned military uniforms out of the corner of their eye. When they turn to get a better look, they find he has vanished. One person described the man as wearing what appeared to be a Civil

Left: Upstairs hallway, site of frequent paranormal activity, Union Station, Ogden. *Photograph by Jennifer Jones.*

Right: Reproduction of the workshop of John M. Browning, John. M. Browning Firearms Museum, Union Station, Ogden. *Photograph by Jennifer Jones.*

War–era uniform and sporting a big moustache. As the museum contains a section of John Browning's military firearms and other memorabilia, perhaps these spectral soldiers have some type of attachment to these weapons and artifacts.

The spirit or spirits that hang around the Browning Firearms Museum have also gained a reputation of patting people on the back or simply touching them on the shoulder. When the visitor turns around to see who it is, no one is there. Some of the volunteers who work in this area feel that it is John M. Browning himself, keeping an eye on his collection.

Even though I don't feel that the basement of the Union Station is one of the most haunted areas, it is the oldest part of the building and, I feel, one of the most interesting. To enter the basement, visitors must walk down some very steep stairs into an often dark area. There are a couple of work rooms in the basement and some narrow utility corridors that branch off in different directions.

Part of what makes the basement so interesting are the six vaults located in the center of the main basement area. The vaults, dating to the 1889 depot, were used to hold valuables that would come in on the trains. Each

John M. Browning Firearms Museum, Union Station, Ogden. *Photographs by Jennifer Jones.*

vault has a heavy steel door with a combination lock on the front. Placed in the center of the room, they were safe from people trying to tunnel in from outside the building. Today, the vaults are used mainly for storage. One is kept locked at all times because it contains museum artifacts that aren't currently on display.

In front of the vaults is the freight scale mechanism that operates the freight scale, located on the floor above, and directly in front of that is the entrance to the basement crawlspace. The crawlspace has a dirt floor and runs directly underneath the lobby of the Union Station. With a flashlight, you can see the original stone foundation from the 1889 building lining either side of the crawlspace. This area has been searched more than once by previous station employees looking for any openings to the tunnel that supposedly ran up Twenty-Fifth Street to the Ben Lomond Hotel.

I have had some strange encounters down here, but I've always felt that they could easily be explained by natural causes. The elevator, for instance, has been known to randomly change floors on its own. Once, while investigating with my team, a few of us were standing in front of the elevator in the basement when we heard it ding. The doors opened, up as if someone had pressed the button. It was definitely creepy, but I always chalked it up to the fact that it was an old elevator that does quirky things.

9

THE GHOSTLY WOMEN
OF THE STATION

On the northern side of the second floor of the Union Station is a long hallway that connects one wing of the building to the other. In the middle of this long hallway is an area that is directly in front of the two-story grand lobby. This area is now used as the Myra Powell Gallery, which hosts art exhibits throughout the year. When the building was still in use as a depot, this hallway allowed staff to get around the vast lobby without having to go downstairs and make their way through the people waiting to board the trains. At that time, the upstairs portion of the station housed offices for the Union Pacific workers, telephone operators and others.

Over the years, there have been many reports of paranormal activity in this hallway. Many paranormal teams have captured EVPs of a woman's voice while investigating the Union Station. Some of these EVPs are very clear; one in particular, captured in this hallway by the PI-Team of Utah, is the raspy voice of a woman saying "Help." People have reported the scent of lilac perfume in this area and the sounds of footsteps behind them. While doing research into deaths that occurred at the Union Depot, I came across a sensational story that made headlines around the country in 1924. It involved a woman who was found dead inside a trunk.

On Wednesday, March 19, 1924, the depot was busy with people trying to get to their destinations, much like any other day. Alexander Brown, who was employed as a baggage handler and electrician for the railway, was busy moving pieces of luggage and cargo off of a train that had just arrived in Ogden from Denver, Colorado. While trying to move a

Myra Powell Gallery, Union Station, Ogden, Utah. *Photograph by Jennifer Jones.*

particularly heavy trunk, Alexander slipped and almost fell to the ground. He soon realized that the liquid he had stepped in was coming from the trunk he was trying to move. Then he came to the realization that the liquid appeared to be blood.

Following protocol, Alexander and the other employees in the baggage area called for an investigator before doing anything further with the trunk. When the investigator for the Union Pacific arrived, the trunk was opened, and they saw what appeared to be the body of a woman with a rug wrapped tightly around her head and tied at the neck. Another rug was loosely wrapped around her torso; women's clothing and newspaper were tucked around her body. The men were horrified at what they were looking at, and the Ogden city police were quickly notified.

While being questioned by police, Alexander Brown mentioned that he thought there was something unusual about the trunk while they were traveling to Ogden, but he didn't give it much thought at the time. He went on to tell police that when he placed the trunk on the train in Denver, he tied an Airedale terrier to it. The dog was being shipped to San Francisco

Freight scale, site of the discovered trunk containing the body of Della Jannsen, Union Station, Ogden. *Photograph by Jennifer Jones.*

by an army officer. He said that the dog clearly did not like being tied to the trunk and incessantly barked and howled. He turned the lights up in the car and said he thought the dog was going mad, that it was trying with all of its might to get loose from the trunk. He thought this was really strange and decided to move the dog to a different area of the train car, away from the trunk. He tied the dog to a different trunk and turned the lights back down. The dog immediately quieted down and remained that way until the train arrived in Ogden.

He went on to say that he realized the trunk this dog had such a strong reaction to was the same trunk that he loaded onto the train in Denver. He said that while he was moving the trunk onto the train, he remarked to a co-worker that it sounded like someone was shipping liquor to California by the way the contents of the trunk sloshed around. According to an article in the *Ogden Standard-Examiner* from March 17, 1924, Mr. Brown remarked to the police, "I kept thinking about the trunk as I took it off the train at Ogden to transfer it to the Southern Pacific for Weed [California]. I slipped, I thought this must be a hoodoo trunk! The dog wouldn't stay tied to it, now I am slipping around handling it. I looked down and I saw a blood spot, a tiny stream of red was trickling out."

Dr. R.H. Wilson, the medical examiner for the City of Ogden, was called, and the trunk with the body still inside was removed to a mortuary not far from the Union Station. Wilson found that the woman was wearing a nightgown and slippers, and from the looks of the clothes she was wearing and the clothing packed around her body, she was not well-off. He determined that the woman died from severe head trauma and that the cause of death was a massive skull fracture. She also had extensive bruising on her arms and throat. Wilson believed that she fought for her life. While this was happening, police were working with Union Pacific officials to find out who had shipped the trunk.

It did not take long for Union Pacific officials to find the name and address listed for the person who shipped the trunk. The name given was John J. Smith, of 4144 Clay Street. The Ogden police detectives decided it would be best if they accompanied the body and trunk back to Denver that night in order to help find who committed this terrible crime. They arrived in Denver late that evening and wasted no time meeting up with the Denver police to start their investigation. Early the next morning, the detectives from both forces began asking around at the Denver train depot if anyone knew of a man named John Smith or a man dropping off a large trunk on Friday, March 14.

As they suspected, they soon determined that the name and address were bogus, but the address, at least, was not far off from the suspect's real address. A few people stated that they remembered seeing a man dragging a heavy trunk and gave police a physical description. The police were able to connect the trunk to Fred Janssen of 4124 Clay Street. They learned that no one had seen Fred Janssen's wife since Thursday, March 13. They knew they were on the right track.

The lady whose body was found in the trunk was Isabella "Bella" Mary Janssen. Originally from Pittsburgh, she worked at a local department store and had been married to Fred Janssen for approximately five years. According to police, based on the condition and quality of her clothing and the items in the trunk, she did not appear to have lived a very easy life.

Police brought Fred Janssen in for questioning, and he started talking right away. First, he told police he was afraid that Bella was trying to kill him and he paid a "Mexican" whose name he could not remember $150 to kill her while he waited in the next room. The detectives were not buying his story, and they soon uncovered evidence that, approximately a month prior to Bella's murder, Fred had taken out two life insurance policies on Bella totaling $1,000. They also learned that after her death he called the Salvation Army to come pick up all of her clothing and other small personal belongings, telling them his wife left him to move back to Pittsburgh with her family.

Finally, after three hours of intense questioning, Fred admitted to murdering his wife. He stated that he hit her over the head with a hammer while she was kneeling at the bed in prayer, strangled her and then stuffed a handkerchief down her throat. The medical examiner stated that she was likely still alive when she was placed in the trunk.

Once locked in a jail cell awaiting trial, Fred Janssen screamed to anyone who would listen that he did not want to die, saying, "Please don't let them hang me." His defense team claimed he was not guilty by reason of insanity. Janssen's trial began on April 8, 1924, with prosecutors seeking the death penalty. His trial lasted less than two days, and it took the jury only eight minutes of deliberation to find him guilty on April 10. Judge Clarence J. Morely stated, "the testimony of a confession was merely circumstantial testimony and as such prevented the infliction of the death penalty." He was sentenced to life imprisonment in Canon City, Colorado, on April 11, 1924. He died in prison at the age of sixty-four on November 29, 1948. He is buried in the Greenwood Cemetery in Canon City, Colorado. The inscription on his tombstone reads "381."

Isabella Janssen wasn't the only woman whose death was connected to the Union Station. Prior to her murder, a chain of events occurred that would end with two people dead and Ogden's Union Station on the front page of newspapers. By 1897, the Victorian station was extremely busy. It was also the height of the era of Electric Alley. Ogden was bustling with people from all walks of life.

Glenna Carter was a young woman who seemed to float between a house of ill repute in Salt Lake City and Electric Alley in Ogden. From all reports, when she would get in trouble with the law in Salt Lake, she would hop on the train and head to Ogden until things calmed down. Glenna went by the name Mamie Evans and was described as being of "slight build, with a wealth of reddish-brown hair, light blue eyes, and would be counted a handsome woman, about 19 years of age."

Mamie had moved to Ogden about a year prior to her death, living at 6 Electric Alley. She was one of the more well-known ladies of the area and was often seen with Dutch Moll and Gold Tooth Alice. She was so popular among the "inmates" of Electric Alley that Ogden police asked her to leave town. Apparently, she would cause such a stir among the men that fights would break out over her attention.

Mamie met John Ross shortly after moving to Ogden. By all accounts, he had become infatuated with her. She, however, did not return his affection, and when she told him as much, he did not handle it well. She made the decision to get out of town and head to Butte, Montana, with a man named Dick Morgan. When John Ross learned that she was leaving town, he became incensed. On more than one occasion, he was overheard saying that he would kill both her and Dick.

On the evening of April 24, 1897, Mamie Evans had plans to meet Dick Morgan at the Union Station to take the 8:20 train for Butte. She knew that John Ross would be lurking around the Union Station and told Dick to not stand close to her and to board the train only well after she had boarded. It didn't take long for John Ross to spot her standing on the platform. He immediately confronted her about her plans to move to Butte. Belle London later told police that she accompanied Glenna to the station and saw Glenna talking with John Ross but could not hear any of their conversation. Accounts from witnesses state that he began arguing with her, demanding to know if she was truly moving to Butte. When she said she was, he wanted to know if Dick was going with her. She said that he wasn't, that she was leaving with her friend and fellow inmate, Lou Binkley, who had come with her to the station.

Not satisfied with her response, he pointed his gun at her and began firing. Mamie immediately started running south on the platform, and the first two shots missed her entirely. In the commotion, John ran after her, firing two more times. The fourth shot managed to hit Mamie Evans directly in the chest, and she immediately fell to the ground. Dick Morgan ran to her side, and her friend Lou disappeared into the crowd. John Ross turned around and ran north on the platform, stopping at the end of the first train car. He put the gun to his head and pulled the trigger, falling instantly to the ground.

Police were a constant presence at the Union Station and immediately began trying to provide assistance to Glenna. Even though she was severely wounded, she refused to name John Ross as her attacker. Both Glenna and John were carried to the baggage room and out of public view. John Ross stopped breathing shortly after being laid on the baggage room floor. Within thirty to forty-five minutes, the horse-drawn hospital wagon arrived to take her to the hospital. According to reports, she remained alive until they reached the corner of Twenty-Fifth and Jefferson, at which point she stopped breathing and was pronounced dead.

The murder suicide made front-page news all over Utah for quite a few days after the incident and was even printed in the *San Francisco Call*. A reporter came from Cincinnati to cover the story and gave Ogden police some background on John Ross. Police would discover a letter in Ross's pocket making it clear that this was premeditated murder. His letter read as follows: "To the Public, I wish to ask the Public to pardon me for the act I am about to commit. I tried to drive it off but I cannot, it must be done sooner or later. I love the Girl with all my Heart, and I can't live without her. I wish that the officers will notify my folks."

One of the peculiar traditions of the era that would be inconceivable today was the viewing of bodies at the morgue by the general public. The bodies of Mamie Evans and John Ross were put on display at Richie's Mortuary the day after the incident. Throngs of people filed through the morgue to satisfy their curiosity and catch a glimpse of the deceased. The newspaper said that the station was also full of people trying to see where the murder had occurred; blood could still be seen on the station platform. Glenna's parents arrived the following day to claim her body and make preparations for her burial.

According to the *Ogden Standard-Examiner*, on the morning of April 26, the funeral for Glenna Carter was held with a "great crowd" in attendance at Ogden City Cemetery. After the publication of this article, however, things get a little murky. One of the great things about doing this type of research in Utah is that most burial records are searchable on a state website. While trying to find the location of Glenna's grave, I found that there is no record of her being interred at the cemetery. I asked people at the cemetery office if they had any record of her burial in the old handwritten records. I was told that they looked by name (including her alias) and could find no record of her being buried there. Unfortunately, Ogden City didn't start keeping official death records until 1898, a year after her murder. After checking with the historians at the state archives, I concluded that there was no death record issued for Glenna Carter. What exactly happened to Glenna Carter is a mystery. I have a feeling, based on all the newspaper reports, that she was buried in Ogden City Cemetery and that her grave was left unmarked and lost to time.

When it came to finding a final resting place for the remains of John Ross, the people of Ogden were not very happy about the thought of burying him in the city cemetery. Ogden police made contact with his aunt in Ohio, letting her know what had happened and asking her to make arrangements for his interment. She let them know that she did not have the money to have his body shipped to Ohio and pay for his burial. Normally, in cases of an unclaimed body or of someone who died with no family and no means to pay for the burial, the deceased was buried at the city's expense in the city cemetery. Ross's body sat at the morgue for a few days while city officials tried to figure out where to bury him. According to the mayor, state statutes prohibited a murderer from being buried in any cemetery within the city limits. Six days after the murder suicide, on April 30, 1897, it was decided that John Ross would be buried in the Poor Farm Cemetery, located outside of Ogden city limits in the small town of Roy. Ross was buried in an unmarked grave.

Since discovering the 1897 murder suicide, I've tended to believe that the shadowy figure often spotted lurking about in the annex by the Browning Theater could be the specter of John Ross. The figure is often reported to move quickly or is seen running down the length of the annex. While many changes to the train platform took place from 1897 to the 1950s, the general location has remained the same.

10

KILLED BY THE CLOCK TOWER

If you ask any of the Union Station staff or volunteers about the ghosts at the station, the story that almost all of them will tell you first is that of the man killed by the falling clock tower. I wanted to see if I could find the name of this man and discover exactly what happened, so I began to research the fire that partially destroyed the Union Station in 1923.

Prior to the current Union Station, there was a large, elaborate Victorian building. Unlike the current building, this one had a few hotel rooms used by employees in the south wing. Its most distinguishing feature and an important part of this story was the large clock tower that loomed above the center of the building. The "new" Union Station opened in July 1889. By all reports, by the early 1900s, the people of Ogden wanted a "modern" station, stating that the station was too small, extremely dark and outdated. Union Pacific, however, did not want to invest money in building a new depot. The station remained as it was until the evening of February 13, 1923.

At approximately 7:00 p.m. that evening, a porter who was staying in the dormitory on the second floor of the southern wing of the building came running into the telephone operator's office to tell the operator there was a fire. The telephone operator later told investigators that she didn't recognize the man. If his identity was ever discovered, it was never made public. It was later determined that this man was pressing a pair of pants and that, when he left the room, he forgot to turn the iron off. It later sparked a fire that would quickly engulf a good portion of the building.

The Ogden Fire Department arrived quickly, and by 2:30 a.m. the next morning the fire was extinguished. Amazingly, there were no injuries or deaths during the blaze. The people of Ogden immediately began discussing the new depot they would finally be getting, and the newspapers and city officials were excited about the possibilities. Their hopes were quickly dashed and excitement turned to anger when Ogden Union Railway & Depot officials announced a few days later that they would not be spending money to build a new depot and would simply repair the damaged building.

While the city and Ogden Union Railway & Depot officials went back and forth about the need for a new station, employees at the station did their best to maintain business as usual. Frank Yentzer was one of those employees. Frank had worked at the Union Depot for four years and had been promoted to cashier only a few months prior to the fire. He had moved to Ogden with his wife and young daughter from Illinois; by the time of the fire, the family had grown to include a six-month-old baby boy. Monday morning, February 26, probably started like any other day for the Yentzer family. Frank would have made his way to the station from his house on nearby Twenty-Eighth Street to begin his duties as cashier. His wife, Helen, would have started her day at home caring for their two young children. The only difference this day was that the cashier's office, instead of being inside the depot, had been moved temporarily to the train platform until repairs could be finished on the interior.

While attempts were made to keep the depot running as smoothly as possible, workers throughout the building were trying to repair the damage. One of the most damaged portions of the building was the large clock tower on the roof in the center of the station. Directly behind the clock tower, located on the edge of the platform, was the façade of the building, which had large, decorative stone finials on both corners near the roof. On that particular day, despite it being fairly windy, a crew of men had been assigned to repair the severely damaged roof. Even though the men were working on an area of the roof that was on the opposite side of the building, not next to the platform full of people waiting to board their trains, a freak accident was about to happen.

Shortly before 2:00 p.m., while the laborers worked to remove a section of damaged roof, a gust of wind blew a portion of the structure free. As it fell, it hit one of the large stone finials, estimated to weigh 250 pounds. The finial came crashing through the skylight of the temporary cashier's office,

Union Station Museums in Ogden, Utah. *Photograph by Tricia Simpson.*

landing on Frank Yentzer, who was sitting directly underneath it. He was killed instantly. Two other men were working in the office at the time; one was slightly injured on the hand, and the other escaped unharmed.

The public outcry after Frank's death finally forced Union Pacific to demolish the damaged depot almost entirely and build a new, modernized station. Within two weeks of Yentzer's death, Union Pacific officials made an announcement that a new depot would be constructed. The new building was just slightly longer than the previous station and used all of the original stone foundation of the first depot, which you can still see in the basement today. The new depot was formally opened on Saturday, November 22, 1924, and hailed as the "gem of the west."

Something interesting about the way the Union Station was rebuilt is that even though the building isn't the exact size and looks entirely different from its predecessor, many of rooms on the first floor are almost identical in location to the layout of the previous station. I was able to find old floor plans of the original station. Areas like the baggage room, restrooms and some offices are in almost the exact same location as in the previous building. This could possibly be part of why many of the paranormal sightings that occur today happen in places such as the lobby, platform and baggage area.

11

PEERY'S EGYPTIAN THEATER

The ghost stories that swirl around Peery's Egyptian Theater are somewhat vague, but they always contain the same element: the ghost of a little girl. The most popular story says that when the theater was being constructed in 1923, a young girl brought lunch to her father who was working on the outside of the building. Depending on the source of the story, the girl fell from one of the theater boxes, fell from scaffolding on the building's exterior or fell out of a window to her death. She is most often described as being a preteen or teenager with shoulder-length brown hair. It is said that her name is Allison, although I haven't been able to track down anything specific as to the source of that name. Theater employees and visitors alike have spotted her, but it seems she is usually seen by those performing on stage. Her ghost has been seen throughout the theater, usually by standing on or near the stairs leading up to the theater boxes. Performers on stage have seen her spinning or playing with a chair in the stage-left theater box. A couple of people have claimed that a young girl was sitting next to them, only to vanish when they looked over again.

Theater employees report unnerving occurrences after the theater is closed and almost empty. Lights that have been turned off for the night will suddenly turn back on. The sounds of someone playing the theater piano have been reported when no one is in the room. And chairs that have been neatly arranged the night before will be in complete disarray when the employees come in the next morning.

Peery's Egyptian Theater. *Photograph in the Carol M. Highsmith Archive, Library of Congress, Prints and Photographs Division.*

I've spent quite a bit of time researching Peery's, trying to track down any historical evidence of a young girl having died there. Unfortunately, I came up empty-handed. I did find an article about a worker being injured during construction of the theater, but no deaths. Even though I didn't find the information I was hoping for, I discovered that the location of Peery's Egyptian Theater has an interesting history. It may be that the ghost of this girl is tied to the site and not necessarily to the theater itself.

Construction on the theater began in 1923 after the previous building at the location burned down. The Arlington Hotel was located at the current site from at least 1909 until it caught fire on March 14, 1923. One of the ads I found for the hotel read, "We wish to announce to the public that our hotel is strictly clean, no bootlegging, gambling nor bad characters allowed. A hotel where you can bring your mother, wife or daughter." Given that the hotel was operating in Ogden during the Roaring Twenties, and that Ogden had such a wild reputation, I found it amusing that the owners of the hotel felt it was necessary to run an ad like that. I did find out that a few deaths occurred at the hotel, all from natural causes: two older gentlemen died in 1911 and 1913, and a twenty-seven-year-old lady died there in 1927.

On the evening of March 14, 1923, a fire broke out at the hotel at approximately 11:30 p.m. By the time the fire department got the blaze under control, the Arlington Hotel, which occupied the upper floor, was almost completely destroyed. A candy store and a department store located on the first floor were also a total loss. Originally, fire officials believed that everyone staying at the hotel had made it out safely. The next day, people began to report that one person who was known to have been staying at the Arlington was unaccounted for.

William Cunningham, or "Bingham Bill," as he was known, had been living at the hotel for quite some time and had been in ill health. When he failed to show up for a doctor's appointment the day after the fire, friends of his began to suspect something was wrong. His body was later discovered, fully dressed and lying in bed. The entire floor he was on had fallen through to the first floor and was covered in debris.

Within weeks of the fire, Harman and Louis Peery, sons of the well-known Ogden businessman and former mayor D.H. Peery and owners of the lot, decided they were going to build a movie palace that would be the "Showplace of the West." King Tut's tomb had recently been discovered, and the Egyptian style was taking the nation by storm. Construction on Peery's Egyptian Theater began in the fall of 1923, and the theater was opened to the public on July 3, 1924. Not only did the theater seat twelve hundred patrons, but it also had a "Mighty Wurlitzer" theater organ (to accompany the silent films) and exquisite Egyptian details. The auditorium ceiling was "atmospheric," and the projectionist could change the ceiling from a daylight sky to a midnight sky complete with twinkling stars. It was also made entirely from poured, reinforced concrete and was advertised as being completely fireproof.

Peery's Egyptian Theater was the highlight of Washington Boulevard for many years, undergoing modifications throughout the years to keep up with the latest technology but also managing to maintain most of its originality. By the 1970s, the theater was run-down, like many other areas of Ogden, and was in desperate need of help. In the 1990s, the Egyptian Theater Foundation was formed and set to work meticulously restoring the theater to its glory days.

It was during the restoration project that the odd occurrences and sightings of the spirit girl began. Maybe she had been there for quite some time but had gone unnoticed until the theater was quiet and empty. Maybe it was the restoration work itself that brought her out, similar to the circumstances at Making Scents on Twenty-Fifth Street. I don't think she died an untimely death at the theater or in the previous hotel, but she most likely has some attachment to the location. It could be something as simple as the fact that she loved going to the theater and decided to hang around, even years after her death.

12
RAINBOW GARDENS

Rainbow Gardens is a unique collection of shops and a restaurant housed in the same building located at the mouth of Ogden Canyon. The building stands adjacent to the Ogden River and a natural spring. Not only does it have the reputation of being quite haunted, but it also has an unusual history. While the management of Rainbow Gardens has remained pretty tight-lipped about the paranormal activity there, I was contacted more than once by people who worked there and experienced unexplained activity.

The first mention I found of people coming to this location was in the *Salt Lake Evening Democrat* in 1885. People would travel to the hot springs at the mouth of the Ogden Canyon to soak in the mineral water. By 1895, a hotel was built on the site that also had a ballroom, restaurant and private mineral baths fed by hot spring water. People began to travel from not only Ogden but also Salt Lake City to visit the Ogden Canyon Sanitarium, and many were sent there suffering from tuberculosis in the hopes that the fresh air and water would help their condition. The building was enlarged numerous times from 1895 until it was finally completed in 1906.

When I start to research the history of a location, I keep my searches pretty broad, and some of the stories I come across are bizarre. One such story involved an incident that occurred in front of the sanitarium on August 6, 1907. A man named William Goda died in a freak accident. Aeronaut Goda, as he was referred to in the local paper, was performing a stunt in which he would ascend in a hot-air balloon and, upon reaching a certain height, jump out with a parachute, aiming to land in front of the sanitarium. The newspaper reported that Goda's balloon reached a height of approximately two thousand feet, and then Goda jumped. Unfortunately, he landed on a power line and was instantly electrocuted.

The first reported death I could find at this site occurred on October 7, 1914, when the body of Ben Taylor, about whom not much was known and whose age was guessed to be about fifty, was found in one of the old concrete swimming pools. A local man searching the area for some cows that got loose happened upon the body and immediately notified police. The police found a gun next to Ben Taylor's body and ruled the death a suicide. In his pocket, they found a scribbled note that read, "Too much asthma. Can't stand."

In 1927, the sanitarium burned to the ground. Only a pile of rubble was left. The following year, the property was sold and renamed "El Monte Springs." It was rebuilt with brick and featured all of the same amenities as before, but with a much larger swimming pool and ballroom. El Monte Springs was incredibly popular in the 1920s as the place to go dancing in Ogden. Unfortunately, it did not survive the Great Depression and closed by 1932. In 1942, the property was purchased by Harman W. Peery, who was known as Ogden's "Cowboy Mayor." Renamed Riverside

Rainbow Gardens, Ogden, Utah. *Photograph by Jennifer Jones.*

Gardens, it once again became a popular destination for swimming and dancing. In 1946, the building was turned over to Harman Peery's daughter, and the name was changed for the final time, to Rainbow Gardens. In addition to the name change, the resort was renovated and eighteen bowling lanes were added.

By 1970, the ballroom was turned into a very large gift shop named Rainbow Imports, and in 1975, the indoor swimming pool was converted to the Gift Garden, selling plants and small gifts. Shortly after these changes occurred, people, mainly those who worked at Rainbow Gardens, began to take notice of odd things. In 1996, the final change took place at Rainbow Gardens—the eighteen-lane bowling alley was turned into yet another shop, Planet Rainbow.

While the management has been unwilling to openly discuss paranormal activity, I was contacted more than once by employees and former employees telling me the location was haunted and asking that my paranormal team come out to investigate. Unfortunately, the management wasn't too keen on the idea; I was never able to investigate Rainbow Gardens. The people who contacted me said that many employees won't go in parts of the building by themselves at night after the shops have closed. They reported a sense of unease in one particular location, the old closed-in porch overlooking the Ogden River. This was the area where those suffering from the effects of tuberculosis would have sat to rest and get fresh air. Employees also reported the sounds of people talking—though they could never make out what was said—as well as labored breathing. Workers also spoke of seeing things move out of the corner of their eye.

13
SHOOTING STAR SALOON

Just through Ogden Canyon lies the small, quiet town of Huntsville. Most people who pass through this town today are usually heading to Pineview Reservoir, which is a popular place to go boating in the summer. Huntsville also happens to be home to the oldest continuously operating saloon in Utah. Not only did the Shooting Star Saloon gain a reputation for a unique atmosphere with great burgers, but it also became known as a place with a few ghosts.

The saloon got its start when Hoken Olsen, an immigrant from Norway, began selling liquor out of what was previously the dry goods store in 1879. He eventually put a sign above the door that read, "Olsen's Saloon, Wines, Liquors, and Cigars." But Hoken never applied for a liquor license, and it didn't take long for city officials to take notice. Over the next sixty-six years until his death, Hoken would be repeatedly charged with selling alcohol without a license. While I was wading through various newspaper articles about Hoken's place, it became clear that the repeat citations didn't seem to bother him, nor did the eventual convictions and even jail- or prison time. It almost seems that it became a kind of game between Hoken and his wife, Maria. When Hoken was convicted and sentenced to jail, his wife would take over the family business until he was released. Maria was cited and convicted of the same liquor offenses more than once.

Around 1903, the city of Huntsville went "dry." Officials tried to shut Hoken Olsen and his saloon down, but he just couldn't be stopped. Once after being released from jail, he told the authorities and the newspaper

Shooting Star Saloon, Huntsville, Utah. *Photograph by Jennifer Jones.*

that he was going into the business of raising and selling chickens. While he might have done that for a short period, he never fully gave up bootlegging or selling liquor without a license, despite every attempt to stop him. To this day, he has the unique distinction of having the most liquor-related citations and convictions for Weber County.

In 1914, Maria Olsen passed away from natural causes at the age of fifty-two. Hoken and their son Clarence kept running the saloon until Hoken passed away in 1945. It appears that Clarence kept a much lower profile than his father. By all accounts, Clarence managed the saloon for some time until it was finally sold to someone outside of the family.

By the late 1970s, people had begun to talk about strange occurrences in the saloon. The stories were initially dismissed as coming from those who may have had a little too much to drink, but they were soon taken more seriously when the same stories began being told by those who worked there.

The saloon is full of unusual artifacts, such as the taxidermied head of a 298-pound St. Bernard, Buck, and the taxidermied head of a jackalope wearing spectacles. In addition, several items found in and around the building during renovations hang above the bar. While not a very large building, it has the original carved wood bar, several booths, an old jukebox and a single pool table.

One of the previous owners (there have only been seven in the last 137 years) did not want employees waiting on tables, insisting instead that patrons order directly at the bar. To help new customers realize this, there are little signs throughout the bar that read, "No waitresses on duty." One night shortly after the owner passed away, one of bartenders went to a booth to take customers' orders. With pen and paper in hand, she began to write down their orders. The pen went flying out of her hand. She told me it wasn't as if she fumbled it, but rather it felt as though someone had grabbed it out of her hand. The staff laughed about it and mentioned that the owner had always promised to come back and haunt the bar after his death.

Some of the paranormal activity in the saloon is centered on the jukebox. When I first heard that the jukebox randomly plays songs, I brushed it off as a feature of an older jukebox. After talking to the current owner, however, I realized that it's a lot more unusual than an old jukebox simply playing songs at random. The owner sat with us in Buck's booth and, under the perpetual gaze of the glass-eyed dog, shared her experiences in the saloon. Shortly after she began talking, the jukebox began to play a song. She said, "Oh yeah, the jukebox! It has a timer and is set to play a song at random every twenty minutes." She told us that people get excited because they've heard the stories and don't realize that the jukebox is on a timer. "That's not the unusual part," she said. "That's what it's supposed to do." She kind of laughed and continued, "You know when something happens regularly, like a song being played every twenty minutes, you tend to get used to it and expect it? Every now and

Inside the Shooting Star Saloon, Huntsville, Utah. *Photograph by Jennifer Jones.*

then it'll play more often than every twenty minutes, and when it does that it seems to somehow relate to something that is happening in the bar, like a conversation that's taking place or an event."

The owner shared a story about a sailor who came to the Shooting Star for a burger and a beer one evening. He had been stationed at nearby Hill Air Force Base and was retiring that day. While enjoying his food, he talked with the bartenders about retiring and how it was a bittersweet day for him. The owner said that, no sooner had he finished eating and was getting ready to leave, the song "Anchors Aweigh" began playing on the jukebox. Everyone sat there stunned for a minute and then laughed it off. The bar was pretty empty at the time, and no one had put money in to select a song or even realized that "Anchors Aweigh" was one of the many records it contained. Given that the jukebox dates from sometime in the 1980s or early 1990s, it doesn't have the capability to connect to a computer or the Internet to have music selections made that way. The owner said that she also heard from the previous owner that the day Ronald Regan died, the jukebox played the same old country song every time the topic of Regan's death was mentioned.

It seems that the activity in the Shooting Star Saloon is very playful in nature. None of the employees or customers has ever felt threatened, scared or uneasy. Lights turning off and on by themselves are also a common occurrence. After the bar has closed for the night and the staff is preparing to leave, they have a routine. They start in the kitchen and work their way around the bar, shutting off all the lights and making sure the front door is locked. The owner said that after they make their way down the side of the bar, switching off the lights at each booth, they then turn off the lights in the restrooms at the back of the building. The backdoor is located off to the side of the restrooms. She said that at least a couple of times a month they will turn to take a final look around before exiting, and the men's room light will be on. They've also opened the bar in the morning to find all of the lights on, even though they were turned off at closing the night before.

A shadowy figure hangs out in the basement and is usually seen toward the back of the building. The owner told me that she has seen it a few times and, while it usually startles her, she doesn't have a fear of going into the basement. She described it as moving very quickly, like a "whoosh" across the width of the basement, passing in front of a doorway and blocking the light that shines from a room in the back. Interestingly enough, Hoken Olsen (and possibly other past owners) would use the basement as a card room, and historical records show that he was arrested at least once for illegal gambling operations. One of the things I have always found interesting about reports of shadow people is the troubling manner by which those who've experienced them try to describe what they've seen. Many seem to have trouble describing how a shadow person appears in darkness. Having experienced this myself, I suggest that it's as if they're darker than the darkness around them. Usually, the witnesses say "Yes! That's it, that's exactly how they look!"

The ghosts of the Shooting Star Saloon don't like to be taken for granted. One night while the owner was cooking burgers, she overheard a conversation between one of the bartenders and a customer. The customer was asking about the ghosts and if the saloon really was haunted. The bartender said that, yes, it was haunted, but that she doesn't really believe in ghosts. Almost immediately after the bartender said that, the container of pepper fell off the shelf and onto the counter. The owner didn't think much of it and put it back on the shelf. She turned around to grab something off the counter behind her, and when she turned back, the salt had fallen off the shelf and was laying on the counter. Now chuckling to herself, she put the salt back in its spot on the shelf and told the bartender to stop saying that the ghosts don't exist. The kitchen is an area with a lot of activity—usually, it's the refrigerator door hanging wide open. Employees will close it, and the next time they come into the room, the door is hanging wide open again. They also smell cigarette smoke in the kitchen area even though there is no smoking allowed in any part of the bar.

I was interested to know if the employees have ever heard anything unusual. I asked if anyone ever reported hearing anything strange or out of place. The owner said that a few times when the bar is empty they'll hear someone whistling a tune in another part of the building. The sound of someone playing a piano has also been heard after hours. There is no piano in the Shooting Star currently, but it did have a piano many years ago.

The Shooting Star Saloon isn't a place that is haunted because of a dark or malicious event. It seems to me that this long-loved old saloon is haunted by those who cared for it throughout the years and are hanging around, either because they loved spending time there or are looking after those who are currently caring for it.

14

OGDEN CITY CEMETERY AND FLO'S GRAVE

The Ogden City Cemetery was created in 1851 as part of the Ogden City Charter. Over the last 165 years, it has expanded to hold 41,916 interments. Next door is the Tiffany Mack Memorial Pet Cemetery. One of the rumors about the pet cemetery is that it served as inspiration for Stephen King's novel *Pet Sematary*. I'll have to admit that, being a big Stephen King fan, I thought this was really cool, until I realized that the Tiffany Mack Memorial Pet Cemetery was created well after King's bestseller was released.

I like to visit this cemetery often. Usually I'm there to do research, but sometimes I go just because I enjoy walking around the cemetery and photographing the interesting headstones that catch my eye. Many of the people I've found while researching the history of haunted places are buried here, some of them in unmarked graves, such as Glenna Carter from the Union Station murder suicide. There are also prominent members of Ogden's past buried here, such as gunsmith magnate John M. Browning and the first principal of Weber State University, Louis Moench.

I'm sure a lot of people think I'm odd for liking to visit cemeteries whenever possible, but I find them fascinating. There is so much symbolism to be found in the headstones, and if you know what the symbols mean, it can give you some clues into a person's life. Many headstones indicate organizations the person belonged to, such as the Freemasons, the International Order of Oddfellows or the Woodmen of the World. And if you take the time to look around and do some research, you'll uncover fascinating stories about people who died long ago.

Some cemeteries, like Ogden City Cemetery, have their own ghost stories. One story focuses on the ghost of a teenage girl. The story of Florence Grange is one of my favorite Ogden ghost stories. This was the first urban legend—or ghost story, depending on who you talk to—that I researched to find out what really happened. After researching stories like this, I often feel as if I somehow get to know who the person was while they were alive. And I really enjoy being able to tell their story, the *true* story. The legend of "Flo's grave," as it is referred to locally, is probably the most well-known ghost story in all of Ogden. When I start talking to people about local ghost stories or my trips to cemeteries, I am often asked about Flo. "Have you seen her?" Unfortunately, I have to answer "No." I have not seen Flo's ghost. But I do know all about her and her legend.

The legend of Flo's grave goes like this: If you visit the Ogden City Cemetery at night and park near Flo's grave and flash the lights of your car three times, her ghost will appear as a greenish mist and float toward you. The legend goes on to explain that Flo died after being struck by a car while waiting for her boyfriend to pick her up for a school dance. Another version says that she died from choking on a piece of candy. I wanted to know how much, if any, of this was true.

Florence Louise Grange was born on November 24, 1903, in Ogden. She was the second child born to Dottie and Ralph Grange. Almost every reference of her printed while she was living refers to her as Louise Grange. From what little information is available, it seems that she was a well-liked girl. There were a couple of mentions of her being a guest at various parties, and she was mentioned as being on the Pingree School volleyball team in 1916.

Florence lived in a small house near Twenty-Ninth Street and Grant Avenue with her parents and four siblings. At the time of her death, she was attending Ogden High. Florence died at 5:00 a.m. on December 29, 1918. She was fifteen years old. The fact that she died in 1918 is important to this legend for a couple of reasons. The first is that cars were not as readily available in 1918 or as affordable then as they are now. A fifteen-year-old with a boyfriend who had a car in 1918 was rare. So the suggestion that she was struck and killed by a car while waiting for her boyfriend to pick her up for a school dance is not very plausible.

In 1918, the world experienced the worst influenza pandemic to date, known as the Spanish flu. An estimated 20,000,000 to 50,000,000 people died from this outbreak worldwide. It claimed the lives of almost 700,000 people in the United States alone, with Utah being the third-hardest-

Grave of Florence "Flo" Grange, Ogden City Cemetery, Ogden, Utah. *Photograph by Jennifer Jones.*

hit state. Unlike normal flu outbreaks, this strain was deadliest to young, otherwise healthy people. By October 1918, most churches, theaters and schools in Utah were closed, with one notable exception. The Ogden School Board made the decision to remain open, and by late November 1918, both hospitals in Ogden were full. City officials turned an LDS assembly hall into an emergency care center. The Spanish flu was spreading so quickly and was killing so many that people were required to have clean bills of health from their doctors just to enter Ogden. From September 1918 to June 1919, more than 2,343 deaths in Utah were reported to have been caused by the Spanish flu.

According to Grange family history, the entire household contracted the flu after one of their tenants became ill and spread it to members of the family. Most of Florence's family seems to have caught a mild case and didn't spend much time sick in bed. Florence, however, was not so lucky. According to the death certificate, she "died suddenly, probably of endocarditis." The contributing factor was influenza. The death certificate also states that she had been sick for ten days. The newspaper announcement of her death mentioned that her body was laid out for viewing in the parlor of her house, as was the custom during that period, before burial in Ogden City Cemetery.

When I realized that Florence Grange had died due to the Spanish flu, it made me wonder how the legend surrounding her grave came to pass. Where did the car connection come from? I've always believed that most urban legends have some grain of truth to them, even if it is a tiny part. It turns out that her father, Ralph Grange, was one of the first auto mechanics in the state of Utah. He was known throughout the state for his knowledge of fixing, building and even racing cars. Interestingly enough, the Grange family home, which is still standing, has an old garage in back that Ralph Grange surely must have worked in for many years.

If you would like to visit "Flo's grave," you can find it at Ogden City Cemetery, located east of Washington on Twentieth Street. Her grave is on Seventh, just north of Martin. You can stop by the cemetery office to get a map of the cemetery and directions to her grave. A word of warning, however: the cemetery closes an hour after dusk and is patrolled regularly at night by the local police.

15

THE HOUSE ON VAN BUREN

I've never told this story publicly before but thought it would be a great one to include, as it happened to me shortly after I moved to Ogden. A few years ago, after going through a divorce, I decided to move to Ogden from a nearby town and needed to find a house to rent. Ogden is full of great, old bungalows that have so much charm, and as someone who loves old houses (the creepier, the better), I was so excited to find one of my own. It didn't take long for me to find one that was close to the downtown area. My two children and I found the perfect house on Van Buren, a little more than a mile and a half from the Union Station. It was a small, three-bedroom, one-bath brick bungalow with a fully finished basement, built in 1927. When I looked at the house before I signed the lease, I didn't get the strange static-electric feel that some haunted locations give me or have any reason to suspect this house would be haunted. However, looking back, when I was saying goodbye to the previous tenants, I remember the lady telling me that she thought I would be happy here, as the house has a good spirit.

We moved into the house at the end of September and settled into our new routine fairly quickly. The first few weeks were uneventful, and I never got the sense that the house might be haunted. Shortly before Halloween, I asked my ex-husband if he would come stay with the kids, as I wanted to go see *The Rocky Horror Picture Show* at Peery's Egyptian Theater with some friends. He agreed and stayed at the house until I returned around 11:30 p.m. He didn't mention anything strange happening before he left that evening.

A week or so later, my parents decided to come for a few days to visit. Because the house was so small, they slept on a pullout sofa in the basement, next to my daughter's room. The stairs leading to the basement were located off the kitchen. The basement had one large, open area and two rooms. My daughter's room was average size, and the other room was very small. It was as big as some walk-in closets. I realized that it was where the homeowners would store coal, complete with an old coal chute. If I had to identify a creepy area in the house, that would be it. I wasn't exactly sure why—it was just an odd room.

My parents are not believers in the paranormal—I think they listen to my stories just to humor me. The third morning of their visit, I was in the kitchen making breakfast, and my dad commented about how late I was up the night before. He wanted to know whom I was talking to in the kitchen at almost midnight. I was puzzled, as I hadn't stayed up late at all. I was asleep by 9:30 p.m., and I hadn't been talking on the phone, especially not in the kitchen in the middle of the night. I explained this to my dad, and he looked a little confused and said, "Well, that is really weird, because it woke me up. I heard a woman in the kitchen, and it sounded like she was having a phone conversation. I just assumed it was you." I figured he had dreamt it. I didn't put much thought into it until a couple of days later.

I was in the bathroom getting ready, and my mom came up to me and asked how my son Zach was doing. Again, I was puzzled. I said, "He's fine, why?" Like my dad had done a couple of days before, she had a somewhat funny look on her face and said, "Huh, I thought so." I asked her again, and she said, "Well, I woke up last night because I thought I heard you talking, and I almost came upstairs, but as I was standing at the bottom of the stairs, I realized that it didn't quite sound like you, so I went back to bed." I said, "You thought you heard me talking?" She said, "Yes, it sounded like you were talking to Zach, so I thought maybe he wasn't feeling well." By now, my curiosity was definitely piqued. I had two of the most skeptical nonbelievers in ghosts tell me they heard a woman talking in my house, in the middle of the night, and I knew it was not me.

After they left, I had a conversation with my ex-husband about how both of my parents told me they heard a woman talking in the middle of the night. He got kind of quiet for a bit and then said, "Huh, that's really strange." He then told me that the night he had come over to stay with the kids, he had fallen asleep on the sofa in the living room and was woken up by a woman talking. He said he lay there for a second to try to make out what she was saying, but he couldn't hear it well enough. When he sat up to investigate, the talking stopped. He said the same thing as my parents did, that it sounded like it was coming from the kitchen.

I decided to do some research on the house. It was built in November 1927 and purchased by Parley Smout. An elderly widower, he lived in the home with his two adult daughters, Ann Frances and Etta Smout. In July 1928, Parley Smout died in the home from old age. The following year, Etta married John McDonald, and they lived in the house along with her sister, Ann, until their deaths. Ann died in the home in 1953, followed by John in 1957 and Etta in 1975.

I didn't live in the home on Van Buren long after that, and in the short time I did live there, I never personally experienced anything strange. I believe that, often, hauntings are simply a type of residual energy left behind after someone passes. Residual hauntings tend to be of people who had strong ties to a location, which I think was the case with this house. It seems to me that my parents and ex-husband caught glimpses of a conversation between two sisters that happened long ago. Or maybe the sisters just wanted someone to know that they're still around, watching over the house and the people who live there.

16

STEED'S POND

Another local urban legend centers on a small pond not too far from Ogden. Steed's Pond, located next to an elementary school in Clearfield, is said to be haunted by a young boy who drowned there in the 1980s. People have reportedly seen his ghost, which stands by the back entrance to the school. When the apparition disappears, all that is left is a small puddle of water and wet footprints leading toward the pond. Like other urban legends, this one gets oddly specific in that it was a fifth-grade boy who attended this school who drowned. The legend never lists a name or a specific year that this happened. Some versions of this story state that the pond was named after the boy who drowned, or that he is returning to the elementary school that he attended when he died, and that is why his ghost haunts that area.

Unlike other urban legends, in which the stories of experiences usually come from a friend of a friend, a good friend of mine related an unusual experience at Steed's Pond. The interesting part is that I hadn't told her about the legend yet, only that I had been there to take some pictures. She told me that one night she was riding her bike on the trail that runs behind the pond. Most of the area behind the pond is fenced, with only a couple of breaks in the chain link for people to get to the trail from the pond or vice versa. To the north of the pond is a line of houses, and to the south of the pond are soccer fields and the elementary school. The pond is surrounded by trees, but most areas are not dense enough to hide in. She said that as she came up to the area of the pond, she heard a noise, looked over to the pond and saw a young boy standing by the edge of the water just staring at her.

Steed's Pond, Clearfield, Utah. *Photograph by Jennifer Jones.*

She couldn't really describe why it made her uneasy, other than that he just didn't seem normal. She said that there was no one else around, that it was dusk and there were no cars in the pond parking lot. She told me that she remembered thinking it was odd that a young boy would be standing there next to the water by himself. She looked away; when she looked back, he was gone, nowhere in sight. She told me that it freaked her out so much that she couldn't get it out of her mind for quite a while and never rode her bike alone on that section of the trail again.

The truth is that the pond wasn't named after a child who drowned there. It was named after the family who owned this land prior to its development. From 1910 to the late 1970s, the Steed family owned many acres of farmland here, including the pond. Sometime in the late 1970s, the land was sold to the City of Clearfield, and Holt Elementary School opened in 1981.

I began my search for information in the 1980s after the elementary school was opened, because if a child from the school had drowned in Steed's Pond, it would have definitely made the papers. After coming up empty-handed, I began to suspect that it was all just legend. But I expanded my search, and a newspaper article from 1949 caught my eye.

On the afternoon of April 22, 1949, three young boys were playing on a small raft in the pond. Two of the boys, Walter and Billy Pacheco, ages nine and ten, respectively, were brothers, and the third was their cousin, Louie Trujillo, thirteen. In 1949, this area would have been fairly rural, surrounded by farm fields.

While playing, something caused the raft to overturn, throwing Walter, Billy and Louie into the water. Billy was able to cling to the raft and make it safely to shore, but Walter and Louie struggled in the frigid water and soon went under. Billy later told authorities that he tried to help the two other boys by extending a paddle, but they were unable to reach it and disappeared beneath the water. Billy ran home carrying Walter's shoes to tell his aunt what had happened and to get help. She quickly returned to the pond with him and repeatedly called out for the boys, but there was no answer, and the water remained still.

Mrs. Trujillo notified the police shortly after 3:30 p.m., and within minutes, authorities were on the scene trying to locate the bodies of the two boys. A rescue crew from nearby Hill Air Force Base made its way quickly to the pond and sent out boats with grappling hooks and long poles to find and recover their bodies. Hours passed, and nothing was found. Finally, at approximately 10:30 p.m., the bodies of Walter and Louis were located and pulled from the water. The two boys had a joint funeral and were buried together in Kaysville City Cemetery.

While I was doing some last-minute research for this book, I found that Walter and Louis were not the only two boys who have drowned in this pond. In September 1967, three boys decided to go for a swim in the pond. Twelve-year-old James Ferguson and his two friends, thirteen-year-old Mike Quintana and fifteen-year-old Grant Woolsey, went to Steed's Pond around 6:00 p.m. At that time, the pond was located near the Steed Dairy Farm. The boys were getting ready to leave and head home when Mike began to have trouble swimming back to shore. He called out for help. James and Grant swam back to help him, and he was able to get to shore safely with Grant. When James began to head back toward the shore, he suddenly had trouble and disappeared under the water. Grant and Mike ran to the nearby dairy for help, and authorities arrived with rescue equipment shortly thereafter. James Ferguson's body was soon recovered in about twenty feet of water. The sheriff's deputy later commented to the local newspaper that it's a little pond that no one is supposed to swim in and that something like this happens almost every year.

17
HOBBS HOLLOW

W hen I first moved to Utah and formed the Northern Utah Paranormal Society, one of the first haunted places I thought about investigating was Hobbs Hollow. I found it on an old website that listed supposed haunted places in each state, and while the story sounded somewhat far-fetched, it also seemed interesting. I was completely new to paranormal investigation and didn't realize all the difficulties of investigating an outdoor location. I also wasn't familiar with the layout of Hobbs Hollow.

Hobbs Hollow, or Hobbs reservoir, as it is sometimes referred to, is a large, manmade reservoir at the bottom of a steep ravine. It's somewhat wooded, and during the spring and summer the area is covered in tall grasses and brush. Even though the hollow is surrounded by houses, they're up on the hill and the area is fairly remote. I decided to check the area out one day and got halfway down the path to the reservoir and noticed signs alerting people to the possible presence of mountain lions. Since I was alone, I wasn't comfortable with the thought of being stalked by a cougar. I decided to explore Hobbs Hollow another day. That was back in 2007, and I didn't think much more about Hobbs Hollow until I started actively blogging about urban legends and haunted history a couple of years ago.

The main ghost story about the reservoir says that in the 1970s a group of people went to Hobbs Hollow for a late-night swim. The water mysteriously became violent, and they were dragged down by the undertow

The reservoir at Hobb's Hollow, Layton, Utah. *Photograph by Matthew G. Jones.*

and drowned. The tale goes on to say that if you visit Hobbs Hollow at night you'll hear people calling for help and see strange reflections in the water.

Hobbs Hollow got its name from the family who settled in the secluded area in the late 1800s. Originally created as an irrigation pond for local farmers, construction of the earthen dam that created Hobbs reservoir began in 1916 and was completed by May 1920. At its greatest depth, the reservoir reaches thirty feet, and people have been warned against swimming here since at least 1943.

The reservoir is not far from Hill Air Force Base, and it was a popular, although forbidden, spot for the local airmen to go for a swim. The first drowning I found mention of occurred here on August 6, 1944. Private William C. Opey and three other men from Hill Field had gone for a swim on a Sunday afternoon. The men stated that they were swimming across the pond when they heard William Opey calling out for help. Private William Smith saw Opey struggling to stay above water and swam back to him to try to help him to shore. He was able to reach Private Opey and began to help him back to shore but became too tired to continue holding them both. Opey slipped under the water and did not resurface. Smith and the other man tried to find him in the water, but being exhausted themselves, they soon went to get help.

The authorities quickly arrived with boats and grappling hooks. When William Opey's body failed to surface and all attempts at locating him were unsuccessful, authorities used dynamite to blast the reservoir in the hopes it would cause the body to become dislodged and float to the surface. Three days later, on Wednesday, August 9, 1944, William Opey's body was finally recovered and sent to Washington, D.C., for burial in Arlington National Cemetery.

Over the next sixty years, at least five more people, all teenagers, would drown in the reservoir at Hobbs Hollow. Joe Junior Munoz, aged sixteen, drowned while swimming with friends on July 26, 1959. Andrew D. Nightengale (sixteen) and Michael Holden (sixteen) drowned under similar circumstances in July 1965 and 1968, respectively. On August 3, 1971, nineteen-year-old Charles Humphrey, a strong athlete, drowned while swimming with two of his friends. The last drowning at Hobbs Hollow occurred in 2004, when an eleven-year-old boy went missing after taking his dog for a walk. His dog was found sitting by the edge of the water, and the boy's body was found in the water, not too far from shore. Since he was by himself, no one is sure what exactly happened that day.

Almost every newspaper article referencing a drowning at Hobbs Hollow includes police statements that "No swimming" signs are posted around the reservoir. Even today, you can find YouTube videos of people jumping off of tree swings into the reservoir. City officials regularly cut down the tree swings and have removed many of the big trees near the shoreline to further discourage swimming here.

I did experience something unusual while visiting Hobbs Hollow recently to take photographs. I was with my boyfriend, and when we got out of our car to walk to the pond, we both had almost fully charged phones. The reservoir is now fenced, and if I remember correctly, there are only one or two small entrances to the pond. I had taken pictures of the area while we were making our way to the pond and had no problems with my phone. My boyfriend had left his phone in his pocket the entire time.

When I walked to the shoreline to take a picture, my phone hesitated for a moment and then completely shut down. When I tried to turn it back on, it gave me the dead battery symbol. I thought that was fairly odd but not totally unheard of, so I asked my boyfriend to take the picture for me.

Standing next to me, he took his phone out of his pocket to take the picture, and his phone did the same thing. It lagged for a minute, and then he noticed his battery was at less than 20 percent. He was able to take a couple of pictures without further problems. When we left the fenced area of the pond and were on the trail headed back to the car, I tried turning my phone on. It turned on immediately and had more than 50 percent battery life.

Urban legends often start as a way to warn others of dangers in certain areas. Over time, they have a tendency to grow and develop a life of their own. There are many ponds around Ogden, and many of them have claimed lives. While doing research, I came across numerous articles about people, usually kids and teenagers, drowning in ponds in and around Ogden. Yet, most of those locations haven't garnered the reputation of being haunted. Maybe there is something to the urban legends after all.

PART II

BRIGHAM CITY

18

CRYSTAL HOT SPRINGS

U tah has numerous hot springs located around the state, but Crystal Hot Springs is the only one I'm aware of that is rumored to be haunted. Located about thirty-four miles north of Ogden, just past Brigham City, there has been a business operating at this spot since the Madsen Hot Springs was established in 1901. Prior to this, however, the hot springs was a gathering spot for the native North Shoshone–Bannock tribe for hundreds if not thousands of years.

The name was later changed to Crystal Hot Springs, and from the mid-1960s to the 1970s, it was owned by the family of a friend of mine. One day as I was talking to her about writing this book, she told me that I should include Crystal Hot Springs because of the experiences that her family had had there. Interestingly enough, as I looked to see if other people had reported it to be haunted, I saw that it was listed on quite a few websites as being a haunted location. My friend scheduled a time for me to sit down with her mother and aunt and talk about their experiences while living at the hot springs.

My boyfriend and I met Cathy and Mary at Cathy's house; I could tell instantly that even though it had been more than thirty years since they lived at the hot springs, the sisters were somewhat anxious to relive their experiences there. In fact, they told me that they had asked other siblings for some stories to share and were told that they really didn't want to think about it, let alone discuss it. Cathy told me how they had paid a visit to Crystal Hot Springs about a year ago and were nervous to set foot inside the lodge because it brought back so many memories of some truly terrifying things that had happened to them there.

Cathy started by explaining that by the time her father had purchased Crystal Hot Springs, she was an adult and was living on her own. But the family had asked her if she could stay at the Hot Springs that summer to keep an eye on things before they moved the rest of the family and household goods in. They had no idea that the property had already had a reputation of being haunted, so she said she didn't think anything of it to stay at the lodge by herself.

One evening, shortly after their family had purchased the hot springs, the two older girls, Cathy and Mary, were sitting at the counter in the snack bar counting money while their younger siblings and some friends were hanging out in the room. As they were counting the money, they heard what sounded like someone walking around in the dance hall, which was next to the snack bar. Thinking that someone had stayed inside the building after they had closed for the night, they got up to see who was walking around in the dance hall, only to find that no one was there. The backdoor—the only way into the room other than the room they had just come from—was locked. One of the girls noticed that this small door next to the stage that led to the attic area was slightly ajar, but they figured it must have been left that way. They didn't think much of it and went back to the snack bar to finish closing up. No sooner had they sat back down and continued their closing duties than they heard footsteps coming from the dance hall again.

They all got up once again, this time a little more creeped out than before, and went to see what was going on in that room. Same as before—there was no one in there. But this time, they noticed that the little door next to the stage was closed. Once again they went back to the snack bar to finish up so they could close for the night. As soon as they began to count the money, they heard the footsteps in the dance hall a third time. They went back to the dance hall, and someone pointed out that the little door was now open again. It was at this time that they got scared and thought that someone was in the building trying to scare them or was up to no good. They ran back to the snack bar, collected all the money and ran up to the house to let their mom know that there must be an intruder in the lodge.

Mary and Cathy, along with their mother and the rest of the siblings who had been at the house, returned to the lodge to search all the rooms and floors to find whoever it was who was sneaking around the building. They searched the basement, the main level with the snack bar and dance hall and the second floor, which had a few bedrooms. They came up empty-handed. They went back to the main floor and were sitting at a table near the entryway talking about how strange the evening had been. They said there were about ten to fifteen people in all; as they were sitting there, they saw a solid black figure run down the stairs, through the snack bar and out the back door. As soon as he was out the door, he completely vanished. Their brothers ran out after it, but there was no one outside. Whatever it was they saw had completely disappeared into thin air.

It was then that they realized that what they had experienced wasn't an intruder—it must have been a ghost. Mary and Cathy later spoke to the son of the previous owner and asked him if his family had ever seen anything odd at the lodge. He acknowledged that Crystal Hot Springs was haunted and that his family assumed it was the ghost of a man who had jumped off the balcony on the second floor and hit the cement below. According to the previous owner, he was a young man who was going to college and worked at the springs over the summer. One night after the hot springs had closed for the evening, he tried to jump off the balcony into the deep end of the pool but missed. He landed on his head, broke his neck and died instantly. The previous owner also told them that another ghost has been heard around the hot springs, that of a child.

After this initial incident, the family experienced numerous strange events in the lodge house at Crystal Hot Springs. Cathy and Mary told me about one bedroom in particular that always had a very negative feel to it. All of the girls of the family and the younger children did not like to even set foot in the room. The room belonged to their brother, and he seemed to handle it well. However, even friends of his who would come over to spend the night would not spend the whole night in that particular bedroom. They reported that the door handle to that room would wiggle as if someone was trying to open the door, and there was the feeling as if something had sat on the foot of the bed. One time, family had come to visit. They hung some clothes in the closet of that bedroom, only to find a couple of hours later that all of the clothes were in a pile on the closet floor.

The upstairs bathroom was also a hotspot for activity, but only for the women in the family. They would be trapped in the bathroom as if the door was locked from the outside. It would usually happen when they were alone in the lodge or were the only ones upstairs. They said they would get so fed up, they'd shout, "Knock it off!" and would then be able to get the door open. They found it very upsetting in the beginning, especially for the younger siblings. The smaller children, who were about eight or nine years old at the time, said they would feel as if someone was following or chasing them in the upstairs hallway. Other than the brother who stayed in that room, the rest of the family tried to avoid that area as often as possible. While they were telling me stories of the activity they experienced there, Cathy mentioned that their younger sister told her she remembers feeling as if whatever it was she felt was chasing her down the hallway of the lodge wanted to stab her in the back. As soon as she said this, I remembered a newspaper article from 1928 that detailed a fight between two men at Crystal Hot Springs in which one was stabbed repeatedly. During the trial, the defendant testified that he had no memory of having a pocketknife that evening, and not a single witness testified to ever seeing a knife during or after the fight. It made me wonder if the children's sense of being chased by someone who wanted to stab them might be some type of residual energy.

One of the most interesting stories from Crystal Hot Springs happened early one winter morning. The family lived in the house near the lodge, but one of their teenage brothers would stay in the furnace room, which was in the basement of the lodge. Not only could he get away from his siblings and have his own space, but it also was the warmest room in the building, as it was heated by the natural hot spring water. One night, he was awoken by the sound of a small child crying. When he got up to look around and see where the noise was coming from, he found that someone was trying to break into the lodge. He called his father, and they scared the person off the property. It wasn't just the family who reported hearing the sound of a child crying. Crystal Hot Springs also has a small camping area, and one morning, a family told Cathy that during the night they were awoken by the sound of a small child crying incessantly. When they stepped out of their trailer, they noticed that other campers had also woken up. They began to look around to try to find where the crying was coming from. They told Cathy that they found some young people sneaking around the outside of the lodge, and when they realized that the campers were watching them, they ran off down the street. They told Cathy it was the strangest thing—as soon as the kids took off down the street, they realized that they no longer heard the crying child. Cathy and Mary said their family felt as if this crying child spirit was looking out for the hot springs, because it always seemed to occur when there was trouble on the property.

My friend's family were not the only ones to experience unsettling activity at Crystal Hot Springs. Other owners, employees and visitors to the springs have reported the sound of footsteps when no one is nearby, doors opening and closing on their own and shadowy figures in the main lodge and near the swimming pools. Those who have seen the shadow figure report it to be in the shape of a man and is a solid shape, not misty or vague. This shadow figure is almost always spotted in the lodge, and it is usually seen from outside when the building is empty and locked up for the night. And even though Cathy and Mary's experiences occurred in the 1960s, I've heard that experiences like theirs are still occurring to this day.

Not surprisingly, while doing research on the history of Crystal Hot Springs, I discovered that there have been a handful of drownings here since it was first opened in the early 1900s. All of those who drowned here were male and ranged in age from four to twenty-six. In 1908, a man's body was found next to the train tracks behind the hot springs. Police were never able to determine who he was, and he was buried in an unmarked grave in Brigham City Cemetery.

19

BRIGHAM CITY TRAIN DEPOT

It seems as if old train depots in northern Utah are a popular spot for tales of paranormal activity. Like the Union Station in Ogden, but on a much smaller scale, the Union Pacific Depot in Brigham City has a reputation for strange occurrences. The depot in Brigham City was actually the site of one of the first paranormal investigations I led with my team in 2007. The volunteers who had worked tirelessly to preserve this historic building were more than willing to open their doors to us and tell us of their experiences.

Opening on May 19, 1906, this depot had thirteen trains departing daily, serving more than six hundred passengers each day. Not only did the depot service passenger rail travel, it also handled freight, including so much local fruit that a cannery was built adjacent to the depot, and it still stands today. Additionally, during World War II, a spur track was built that ran from the depot to the newly constructed Bushnell Army Hospital located near the mouth of Sardine Canyon. All of the wounded soldiers being sent to Bushnell for their specialized services passed through Ogden's Union Station first, then on to the Brigham City depot to be put on military trains headed to Bushnell.

Walking through the front door, you come to the ticket office, which remains fairly unchanged from when the depot was built, including the original telegraph desk. The room on the north side of the building was originally the women's waiting room, and the room on the south side was the men's waiting room. A freight room was later added next to the men's waiting room.

Historic Brigham City Depot Museum, Brigham City, Utah. *Photograph by Jennifer Jones.*

Volunteers at the depot said that seeing shadow figures was a common occurrence while they were alone in the building. Usually spotted out of the corner of their eye, the figure would be seen passing in front of one of the doorways to the old waiting rooms. At first, they said they figured it was someone coming to visit the museum. The volunteer would walk over to greet them but find that there was no one there. Because it is an old building with a heavy front door and squeaky wooden floors, it is pretty difficult to walk around the museum without being heard. After a while, they said they just quit getting up to look because they knew that no one would be there.

The sound of footsteps is another frequent occurrence in the building, usually heard in the freight room or coming from the attic above. Hearing someone walking around in the attic is unsettling given the history of the building. When the depot was constructed, it was intended as living quarters for the station agent. At some point, he decided he didn't want to live at the depot, so the attic was left mostly unfinished. To get to the attic, you must climb a steep ladder and then lift yourself onto the attic floor. From personal experience, I can say that it's not terribly easy to get up there. Currently, the attic is used as storage space, accessed by staff infrequently. While they initially said the sounds of footsteps in the attic was somewhat startling, they've become used to it over the years and shrug it off as just a quirk of the station.

During our investigation, as we were conducting EVP work in what was the ladies' waiting room, we heard what sounded like a sigh or someone whispering. Upon playback of the audio, we could hear not only the sigh but also our reactions to it. At the end of our investigation, while putting equipment away, fellow investigator Julie Meadows and I smelled the faint scent of pipe tobacco. No one on the team at the time was a smoker, and since it was well after 1:00 a.m., there was no one in the immediate area outside the depot.

The Brigham City Depot is one of the haunted places in northern Utah that doesn't seem to get much attention from the local paranormal community. I've heard people quickly dismiss it as "not that haunted," whatever that means. This could be partially due to the fact that it's on the outskirts of a fairly small city, or perhaps because it doesn't have any tragic events connected to it. The closest thing I could find to anyone dying at the depot was mention of a Union Pacific worker's body found just north of the depot after being bisected by the wheels of a train in 1945. It was never determined if the man committed suicide or was just the victim of a freak accident.

Simply because a location doesn't have a history of tragedy shouldn't cause investigators to immediately write off tales of paranormal activity, especially when they're coming from those who work there and spend a lot of time at the location. The Brigham City Depot was of major importance to the town during its lifespan. People spent a lot of time in the station, either working there or simply passing through, and I imagine that there were a few people who really loved being in the station, especially those who worked there for many years. Many locations are thought to be haunted by people who spent a lot of time there and by those who had an emotional attachment to the location. I think this is the most likely explanation for the ghosts of the Brigham City Depot.

20

BUSHNELL ARMY HOSPITAL/
INDIAN SCHOOLS

When I started writing about the haunted places of northern Utah, I was excited to be able to share my experience with the Bushnell Army Hospital, more commonly known as the Brigham City Indian Schools. Every state has at least one haunted location that is a "must see," and the Brigham City Indian Schools was that place for Utah. One of the reasons why it was such a big deal for those who were interested in the paranormal to investigate the site is that no one was ever given permission to investigate there that I am aware of. You couldn't even set foot on the property without fear of being cited for trespassing.

Shortly after moving to Utah, I was driving through Brigham City heading toward Logan. I noticed derelict buildings off to the side of the highway. They all looked the same: tan brick with green roofs and boarded-up windows. I thought they looked incredibly interesting, even spooky in a way. I had absolutely no idea what they were, and for a couple years, I didn't give them a second thought.

One day while talking to my friend Helmey about haunted places in Utah, he mentioned the Brigham City Indian Schools and how it was the one place in the state he really wanted to get into and investigate. It was then that I realized he was talking about all of those buildings I had seen that day, and it then made sense when I realized that on the side of the mountain opposite the Indian Schools is a large white *I*. He then went on to tell me how, because of so much trespassing and vandalism over the years, it's practically impossible to get permission to investigate the place. He wasn't even sure who actually owned the property.

Former dormitory buildings of the Intermountain Indian School, Brigham City, Utah. *Photograph by Jennifer Jones.*

I want to take a moment and point out that this is one of the reasons why I hate when people trespass haunted locations. I have never trespassed anywhere in order to brag about being at a location. Not only is it illegal and can often be dangerous, but it also ruins potential haunted locations from being investigated by decent people and paranormal teams. More than one place in Utah has been closed to any investigations due to repeated trespassing and vandalism. You'd be surprised at how many locations will actually give you permission to investigate if you go about it the right way.

As I was talking to Helmey about the Indian Schools, he told me that it had first been a hospital during World War II. There had been rumors of odd experiments taking place there. He didn't know specifics but had heard that many of the experiments were of a psychiatric nature. More current rumors hinted at the abandoned buildings being used for satanic rituals and that there was blood on the walls and strange graffiti inside. There were also stories of strange things occurring in the empty buildings, such as doors slamming shut behind people, disembodied voices and things being thrown at those who had illegally ventured inside. It sounded like a lot of hype and typical urban legends to me, but

Looking east toward the canyon. View of the former dormitory buildings of the Intermountain Indian School, Brigham City, Utah. *Photograph by Jennifer Jones.*

by then my curiosity was more than piqued and I wanted to find out as much as I could.

I found that construction of what was originally referred to as the U.S. General Hospital began in May 1942, and the official name of the hospital, Bushnell General Hospital, was announced on July 7, 1942. Apparently, before the hospital was even completed, there was fear among the residents of the small town of Brigham that the hospital would house large numbers of psychiatric patients. The hospital commander, Colonel Robert M. Hardaway, announced, "The hospital is being built to accommodate all types of patients with all manner of ills such as ordinary routine hospital cases are experienced in all army hospitals." He went on to squash another rumor: that there were underground passages, subways or basements and that all buildings would be connected by walkways.

When completed, Bushnell had sixty-three buildings and cost more than $9 million. On October 10, 1942, the hospital accepted its first patients, who were transferred from Hill Field. Within a year, the hospital had accepted more than 8,478 patients from every theater of war. The number of patients Bushnell had treated in that year was more

Vacant buildings at the former Intermountain Indian School, Brigham City, Utah. *Photograph by Wikicommons user Ntsimp.*

than the entire population of Brigham City. At the time, Bushnell was the fifth-largest military hospital in the world, with the capacity to hold 2,000 patients. It specialized in amputations, plastic surgery, treatment of malaria, neurology/neurosurgery and psychology. It was one of the first medical facilities to experiment with the use of penicillin and plastic prosthetics, and it had state-of-the-art X-ray capabilities.

While combing through death certificates in Brigham City from 1942 to 1946, I found that at least ninety-three people had died there. Most of those who perished died from diseases or injuries that occurred during combat. Bushnell also held German and Italian prisoners of war. They lived at the hospital and performed a variety of jobs at the facilities. Prisoners of war who perished here were buried in Fort Douglas Cemetery in Salt Lake City. A very small percentage of the deaths here were due to suicide, and I found at least two murders that occurred at the hospital, both committed by patients.

Because the hospital was so prominent, it attracted a lot of attention from celebrities and other well-known people. Among the famous people who

Bushnell, Indian School. *Photograph by Panoramio user chetross68.*

visited the hospital were the following: Helen Keller, Harry S Truman (prior to becoming president), Nat King Cole (who performed for the patients in the psychiatric ward), Clark Gable, Bob Hope and Shirley Temple. Hope and Bing Crosby actually organized a fundraising concert in Salt Lake City to raise money for a golf course at Bushnell, but unfortunately, the hospital was closed before the golf course could become a reality.

Although the government had initially intended for Bushnell to serve as a hospital for many years, when the war ended, it became clear that it wasn't cost effective. The closing of Bushnell General Hospital was announced on April 4, 1946, and all patients and staff would be out of the city by July 1, 1946. In the four years that it was an active hospital, over thirteen thousand patients were treated.

The old hospital sat empty for the next three years, and in August 1949, the Department of the Interior announced that the buildings would be turned into the Intermountain Indian School. Created by a federally funded program, the school was intended to help educate Native American students, mainly those from the Navajo reservation. Rather than build schools on the reservations in Utah, Arizona and New Mexico, the Intermountain Indian School was created to function as a vocational boarding school. On January 11, 1950, the first students arrived at the school, bussed from Fort Defiance,

Arizona. At the peak of enrollment, the number of students topped twenty-three hundred, making it one of the largest Native American boarding schools in the United States.

The school's purpose was to provide a better education for Native Americans, who, historically, had poor educational opportunities on the reservations, and also to assimilate them into the mainstream American culture. Not only did they have to speak English while at the school, but they also had to dress in the typical teenage American style. The school taught not only basic subjects but also vocational skills such as auto mechanics, welding and painting for the boys and homemaking, cooking and sewing for the girls. The children would live at the school for the entire school year and would be bussed back to the reservations for the summer.

From many accounts, the Intermountain Indian School was thought to be a success in that it helped create greater opportunities for many Native Americans. I have heard from many of those who attended the school, and they had nothing but positive memories from their time there. However, by the early 1970s, Navajo leaders began to push for educating their children closer to home. The Indian School stayed open through the 1970s by accepting students from other tribes, but finally, in 1984, the doors of the school were closed for good.

As the years went by and I investigated various locations across the state, I always kept the Indian Schools at the top of my list of places to investigate. Then one day, Helmey called me to tell me he saw an article that said the Indian Schools were going to be torn down. We figured it was now or never, and we also now knew that the property was currently owned by Utah State University. I am kind of a wimp when it comes to trying to get into locations, so I found a contact at Utah State, gave the information to Helmey and crossed my fingers.

A week or so later, while at work, I got a call from Helmey saying that he was given permission to investigate the Indian Schools, but we had to go there right away. Thankfully, my employer knew about my penchant for weirdness and let me leave early that day. Helmey originally didn't have plans to drive the two hours to Brigham City, so I called Robert, a friend with whom I had been investigating since 2007. We knew this was a once-in-a-lifetime experience, and we immediately headed to Brigham City.

It was early December 2012 on a cold and windy day. We got to the Indian Schools around 1:00 or 2:00 p.m. and met our contact on the street near one of the buildings. I hadn't realized that demolition had already started and was saddened to see that many of the large buildings were

Exterior of abandoned dormitories, Intermountain Indian School, Brigham City. *Photograph by Jennifer Jones.*

already gone. I could tell that our contact thought we were kind of crazy to go to all the trouble of coming out and walking through buildings that had been sitting empty for the last thirty years, but we explained to him that we wanted to document what was left before they were gone forever. When I asked why they were tearing them down, he said it was to make room for a new Utah State campus but that they planned to keep one of the buildings and turn it into a museum about Bushnell and the Intermountain Indian School. After showing that we had purchased reflective vests and hardhats, had medical insurance and signed release of liability waivers, we were given full permission to enter any of the remaining buildings that weren't currently being demolished.

I called Helmey and told him he was crazy and would regret not being here. I told him to hurry up and get to the Indian Schools. Robert and I set off for the nearest building and realized that most windows and doors were still boarded up. Just gaining access to the building was going to be a challenge. We spotted a building where a boarded-up window had been partially pulled off, and we were able to climb through the window and into the building. Once inside, we soon realized that the buildings, which appeared to be fairly solid from the outside, were completely rotting away on the inside. Years of neglect, vandalism and exposure to wind, rain and snow had taken a major toll on the structures. The cost to try to repair the buildings would have been astronomical. As someone who has a love and respect for historic buildings, haunted or not, I hate to see them torn down. But in this case, I knew that they were too far gone to be saved.

Robert and I began to explore the first building and realized that in our haste we forgot to bring something as basic as a flashlight. I've investigated abandoned locations before, and while the possibility of spotting a ghost doesn't scare me, the thought of running into the living in an abandoned place is not one of my favorite things. Thankfully, it hasn't happened to me yet! I began taking pictures of everything as we walked around. We found that there were areas where the floor had completely rotted away. One misstep would send you down about ten feet into a basement full of debris.

There were long, dark hallways with numerous rooms lining either side. Many of the rooms still had some furniture in them; some had curtains on the windows. It was eerie, to say the least. We found what appeared to be old classrooms with chalkboards still on the walls, covered in graffiti. It was strange: a few hundred yards away there was a small crew of construction workers hauling debris from the building they had razed, but the building we were in was silent other than the occasional sound of dripping water.

Decrepit interior dormitory hallway, Intermountain Indian School, Brigham City. *Photograph by Jennifer Jones.*

Interior hallway, Intermountain Indian School, Brigham City. *Photograph by Jennifer Jones.*

Elevated walkway connecting dormitories, Intermountain Indian School, Brigham City. *Photograph by Jennifer Jones.*

Entering a stairwell, we found papers strewn everywhere. When I reached down to see what they were, I noticed that most were dated to the early 1950s and were announcing the start of the school year. Finally, Josh arrived, and we continued walking through every building we could get into. A few times while walking down a hallway we would hear noises coming from other parts of the building that sounded like someone was inside—a door closing, something being knocked over or footsteps. We would stop to listen, and the noises would also stop. We thought maybe someone was in the building with us, but we never ran into anyone, and when we went outside, the closest people we could see were yards away.

We finally decided to pick a spot and spend some time doing EVP work. In the middle of one of the buildings in a large open room, we sat down with a voice recorder and decided to start talking about the history of the site. Over the years, Helmey and I found that we got better results with EVPs when we sat down and had a conversation with each other about the history of a location, any interesting events that occurred there and the people involved, instead of just asking simple questions, such as, "Is anyone here with us?"

I focused mainly on the four years when the buildings were used as a hospital, because that was the period when the most traumatic events and

Right: Interior dormitory hallway, Intermountain Indian School, Brigham City. *Photograph by Jennifer Jones.*

Below: Modern view of Intermountain Indian School site, Brigham City, Utah. *Photograph by Jennifer Jones.*

all of the deaths occurred. We talked about the war and the injured soldiers who were brought here, the doctors and nurses who treated the patients and the rumors of possible psychiatric experiments that were conducted at Bushnell. While sitting on the floor in the center of this large, open room, we heard what sounded like two men talking and movement outside one of the open doorways. Robert immediately got up to go see who was out there, but there was no one nearby and no way that they could have gotten far enough away to not be seen without making noise. We continued our EVP session for a few minutes longer, but as it was getting dark and was freezing cold, we decided it was probably time to wrap it up and find our way out of the building.

Later that week while reviewing the audio we had recorded, we found we had captured the voice of a man saying "Hello?" Right after the voice is heard, we all stated that we thought we heard and saw something; Robert left to check it out. This is hardly conclusive evidence that the old Indian School was haunted but interesting nonetheless.

Within a week or so of our visit to the Indian School, the remaining buildings were demolished, except for a handful that have been converted into other businesses and apartments. Regardless of whether or not the old Bushnell General Hospital/Intermountain Indian School was haunted, it's impossible to deny the historical significance these buildings had on Brigham City and the people who lived there.

PART III

LOGAN AND SMITHFIELD

21

THE NUNNERY

Hidden in the woods along the winding road through Logan Canyon is a group of cabins known locally as the Nunnery. What began as a family's small summer retreat in the early 1900s has gained the reputation over time as one of the most haunted locations in northern Utah. When I started to sort through the history and stories of the location, I found that there were so many different rumors about what had occurred here that it was difficult to find where it all began.

The most often repeated rumor about the Nunnery claims that the Catholic Church sent nuns here if they became pregnant so that the church could keep the pregnancies secret. The babies would be delivered in secret and then placed for adoption, with none the wiser. As the story goes, in the 1940s, one nun decided to run away with her newborn baby in the middle of the night. When the mother superior found out that the nun and baby were missing, she ran into the woods after them. It is said the young nun hid her baby under some brush and headed off in another direction in an attempt to distract the mother superior and keep her from the baby. After hiding in the dark for a few hours, she returned to the spot where she had hid the baby, only to find the baby missing. She headed back to the nunnery grounds and found that her baby was floating face down in the swimming pool. Distraught and heartbroken, the nun committed suicide that night, and the incident was kept secret for many years. Another version of the story claims that two nuns got into a fight by the pool and one pushed the other, who fell and hit her head on the edge of the pool, killing her instantly.

Rumors of the events started to make their way around town and eventually throughout northern Utah that the Nunnery was one of the most haunted locations in Logan. People claimed to have seen the ghost of a young child throughout the property, shadow figures have been spotted inside and outside the buildings, ghostly nuns have been seen walking the property and the sounds of a baby crying have been heard in the middle of the night.

After the Nunnery was abandoned, people tried to sneak in so that they could possibly experience the paranormal activity for themselves, something often referred to as "legend tripping." This only caused the rumors to grow, and more people began to flock to the site after dark, trespassing and often vandalizing the property, causing large amounts of damage. Police began to patrol the area looking for trespassers and citing any who were caught. Because the story behind the haunting sounded so extreme and farfetched, I had to try to get to the real history of the Nunnery and find out what really happened here. What I found wasn't as extreme as the rumors, but interesting nonetheless.

The Nunnery got its start as Hatch's Camp, which was a small cabin built on this site sometime between 1915 and 1918. Hezekiah Hatch was a prominent Logan businessman and the head of Logan Bank. The Hatch family would spend summers in the cabin enjoying the fresh air, the nearby river and the seclusion of the surrounding forest. Over the years, other cabins were added to the property, and it was eventually passed to Hezekiah's son L. Boyd Hatch sometime in the 1930s.

During the years that L. Boyd Hatch and his brother-in-law Floyd Odlum owned the property, it gained the reputation of being one of *the* places to vacation if you were wealthy and well connected. L. Boyd Hatch lived in New York and made his fortune from insurance, real estate and investments. Floyd Odlum, one of the ten wealthiest men in America in the early twentieth century, was well connected and close friends with Amelia Earhart, financing most of her early flying activities. The Hatch and Odlum families would fly or take the train from New York to Utah and spend summers at Hatch's Camp, often bringing with them celebrities and other powerful people from that time. Marilyn Monroe and Joan Crawford are just two of the celebrities that I could verify who spent time at Hatch's Camp.

In September 1951, the Hatch family donated the camp to the Catholic Church through the St. Thomas Aquinas Parish in Logan. The church changed the name to St. Ann's Retreat and used it as a place for the nuns and other members of the church to rest and relax. While owned by the

Catholic Church, it was also used as a summer camp for disadvantaged youth. The kids would be bussed to St. Ann's for a week in the summer, and from the few mentions I could find in the newspaper, it was something that the kids looked forward to every summer. By 1978, the camp was in need of major renovations and was abandoned by the church. It has sat empty ever since. Throughout the years, the camp has been sold a few times to private owners, all in the hope of bringing it back to life. As of today, however, the camp is still empty and in disrepair.

People still flock to the Nunnery, sneaking onto the grounds in hopes of catching a glimpse of a ghostly nun or the shadow figures that are reported to roam the area. Whether or not the location is actually haunted or just a victim to legend tripping is hard to say. Not very many paranormal groups have been given access to the location over the years. Many of those that have visited, however, say the place feels "off." They report the feeling of being watched and followed and said that the place seems ominous.

22

THE MAIN THEATER

The Main Theater is located just north of Logan in the small town of Smithfield, Utah. What appears to be an unassuming old theater on the outside turned out to hold one of the most interesting paranormal experiences I've had so far. I don't remember the specifics as to how we became aware that the Main Theater was haunted, but we called the current owner, and he was willing to let us spend some time in the building.

The owner and people who spent a lot of time at the theater reported strange occurrences there, usually when the theater was closed and mostly empty. Among the reported phenomena were unexplained noises in the building, footsteps, doors closing and disembodied voices. Shadow people were also reported, usually around the stage area and in the projection room.

The theater was built around 1897 by John Hillyard. Mr. Hillyard was married to Theresa Merrill Hillyard, and they had five daughters. This building has been known by many names in the 119 years it's been operating: Hillyard Opera House, Hillyard Theater, Hillyard's Hall, Hillyard's Show House, the Globe Theater and, finally, the Main Theater. Hillyard's Hall was the first large community building in Smithfield, and it was also the first building to have electricity and electric light fixtures in the town. According to Glen Thornley, a local historian, the building is located approximately one hundred yards north of the northeast corner of the old Smithfield Fort. Also, the first Smithfield jail was located directly behind where the theater now stands.

In the early years of the theater's history, it was used as the local meeting hall for church events, dances, boxing matches, vaudeville shows and even as a roller-skating rink. In 1919, the theater was first used to show motion pictures, and it retained that capacity until sometime in the late 1960s or early 1970s. After that, it sat empty for many years until it was sold in the 1990s and began to be used for theater events again.

On a frigid night in January 2008, my team and I made our way to Smithfield to investigate the theater and see if we could find any evidence of paranormal activity. We started by talking with the owner about his experiences in the

The Main Theater, Smithfield, Utah. *Photograph by Jennifer Jones.*

building while he gave us a quick tour. He told us that he had heard a rumor that a man had been crushed to death when the boiler was being installed in the basement many years ago, and the people who worked in the theater did not like to be in the basement by themselves. The other area where a lot of activity occurred was the projection room. He said that people would often hear voices and that a shadow figure had been spotted in that area on more than one occasion. Based on his stories, we decided to start our investigation in the two areas with the most activity, the projection room and the boiler room.

Throughout our investigation of the Main Theater, we were plagued by equipment problems. One member of our team was conducting an EVP session in the boiler room when she said she felt like something grabbed her ankle and then her voice recorder shut down and wouldn't turn back on. As soon as she came upstairs, the voice recorder turned right on. We had a similar occurrence while sitting near the projection area—our video camera would simply turn off. We would turn it on, and it would run for a few minutes before turning off again. The strange part was that it wasn't indicating that the storage card was full or that the battery was dead. It was as if something was turning it off. It's interesting to note that we didn't have any issues with the video camera in the other parts of the building. We also experienced battery drain on a different voice recorder in this area and recorded unexplainable temperature fluctuations here.

We captured two very clear EVPs during this investigation. The first was the voice of a little girl saying quite clearly "No" when we asked if we were intruding on whatever was haunting the theater. The second is one of the creepier EVPs I've captured. While in the boiler room, two of the investigators were having a conversation while a voice recorder was running. Upon review, a male voice clearly says, "I am wise" in the background of the conversation. What it means, I have no idea, but it is definitely one of the most unusual EVPs I've come across.

The most interesting part of this investigation took place when I was least expecting it. We had been at the theater for a few hours and decided to call it a night. While the rest of the team was on the main floor packing up most of the equipment, I decided to head upstairs to the projection room and turn on the lights of the building. I went up the stairs. In order to get to the projection room, you have to walk past what looks like a small closet with no door. As I passed by the open doorway, I saw what looked like a young girl huddled in the back of the closet. She looked to be no more than seven or eight years old, sitting with her knees pulled up to her chin and her head down. She was wearing a light yellow or cream-colored dress, had long brown hair partly pulled up with a light-colored or white bow. Her bangs were covering her forehead, and her face was hidden by her knees. She had white socks that were folded at the cuff, with off-white patent leather shoes that were scuffed and dingy. I passed by the closet so quickly and focused on turning the lights on that it didn't fully sink in that she shouldn't be there until I was a few steps past the closet. I quickly turned around for a double take, but she was gone.

The most unusual aspect of what I witnessed was that she appeared to be solid, not transparent in any way. In fact, when I walked past the closet, I couldn't tell that old film canisters were stacked against the back wall. This apparition had completely blocked them from my view. I immediately had questions, such as, Who was this little girl? Why was she hiding in a closet? Why did she wait until we were leaving to show herself? Unfortunately, I didn't find any proof that might answer the questions I was asking. I found nothing that could help explain why a little girl could be haunting the theater. I also found no reports of a man being crushed by the boiler.

In the nine years that I have been actively investigating the paranormal, this is the only time I have witnessed a full-bodied apparition, and it occurred in the most unlikely place. At that time, the Main Theater wasn't known as a very haunted location. I haven't been back in the years since to see if the little girl is still around, although I do know that other investigative teams have picked up some of the activity at the theater.

23

WEEPING WOMAN OF
LOGAN CITY CEMETERY

I've always found Logan City Cemetery to be interesting, partly because it's in the middle of the Utah State University campus. It's also rumored to be haunted, and one grave in particular is where all of the activity is said to originate. I should say that I've never been a fan of investigating cemeteries. I feel that, normally, when a place is haunted it's because someone had a real affection for the location, spent a lot of time there or suffered a tragedy. Cemeteries to me don't really fit any of these circumstances, in most cases.

The first burial in Logan City Cemetery took place in 1865. It's a pretty large cemetery, with approximately 17,600 interments to date. The grave of the Weeping Woman is located almost in the center of the cemetery and is so large that it's not difficult to find. Many times, such as with Flo's Grave in Ogden City Cemetery, the legend surrounding the haunting doesn't have much in common with the story of the person who is buried there. The sad tale of the Weeping Woman, however, fits with the circumstances of the woman's life and death.

People say that if you visit Logan City Cemetery at night, preferably while there is a full moon, the monument of the Weeping Woman will appear to be crying, and you'll hear what sounds like a woman weeping. I've had people tell me that they visited the cemetery to see for themselves and were shocked to find that, indeed, water was falling from the face of the statue—on a night when there had been no rain. Others have told me that, while cutting through the cemetery to get to their dormitory or other building on campus, they've heard the sound of someone weeping and

Left: The Weeping Woman, Logan City Cemetery, Logan, Utah. *Photograph by Jennifer Jones.*

Right: Detail of the Weeping Woman, Logan City Cemetery, Logan. *Photograph by Jennifer Jones.*

decided to get out of the cemetery as quickly as possible. It sounds like just another local legend, right? Maybe, though, there's more to this legend?

The Weeping Woman monument is a ten-foot-tall granite statue that was erected to the memory of a woman named Julia Emelia Cronquist, who died on January 8, 1914. Julia was married to Olif Cronquist, one of the first county commissioners in Cache County and a prominent dairy farmer. They had eight children during the course of their marriage, but only three survived to adulthood. Their first child, Margaret, was born in 1880, followed by boys Olief and Oliver in 1883 and 1885, respectively. Another son, Orson, arrived in 1888, and everything was going well for the Cronquist family. In March 1889, a bout of scarlet fever struck the Cronquist household, and Olief succumbed on March 22, followed three days later by his brother Oliver. This is also mostly likely when Julia contracted scarlet fever, which caused her to have heart problems for the rest of her life and led to her untimely death.

Julia and Olif went on to have four more children: Elam in 1892; Lilyen, who was stillborn, in April 1894; Emelia in 1896; and Inez, who was born in 1899. From all accounts, the family was happy, and Olif and Julia were well-respected members of the community. The happiness was short-lived, however, when scarlet fever struck the family for a second time in February 1901. On March 1, 1901, the two youngest children, Emelia and Inez, who were four and two, respectively, at the time, succumbed to the effects of scarlet fever.

Within a matter of twelve years, Julia and Olif Cronquist had lost five of their eight children. After this, it is said that Julia Cronquist would make almost daily trips to Logan City Cemetery in her surrey to sit at the graves of her children and mourn. The following years were not kind to Mrs. Cronquist, who was frequently ill with rheumatic fever, a side effect of her previous bout with scarlet fever. On January 8, 1914, at the age of fifty-two, Julia died from valvular disease, caused from "several attacks" of rheumatism. The people of Logan usually said that Mrs. Cronquist died of a broken heart. In August 1917, Olif Cronquist had the Weeping Woman monument erected at the family burial plot in honor of his late wife. It was made out of Barrie granite and was created by one of the finest stone carvers in all of Utah. The monument was so large and beautiful that mention was made of it in the *Logan Republican* on August 9, 1917.

While it's a compelling story that the Weeping Woman cries tears, upon closer inspection of the face, you can see where water runs down the head of the statue, along the side of the nose and onto the face. If you were to visit the area shortly after it had rained, it would be easy to see how this could be viewed as the statue crying tears. But I'm not so sure about the claims of hearing a woman weeping in the middle of the night. Perhaps the ghostly cries of Mrs. Cronquist are residual energy that happens to replay every now and then as if recorded on a loop. If you find yourself in the cemetery at just the right time, you might hear a glimpse of her heartbreak from many years ago.

BIBLIOGRAPHY

Books

Browning, John, and Curt Gentry. *John M. Browning, American Gunmaker*. New York: Browning, 2012.

Dunning, Linda. *Specters in Doorways*. Alton, IL: Whitechapel Productions Press, 2003.

Roberts, R.C., and R.W. Sadler. *Ogden Junction City*. Northridge, CA: Windsor Publications, 1985.

Magazine Articles

Hoffman, Glenda. "Ghost Tours Explore Ogden's Paranormal Hotspots." *Signpost* (October 24, 2013). Weber State University.

Hunter, Jeff. "Pine Glenn Cove: The Real Story Behind 'The Nunnery.'" *Cache Valley Magazine* (September 2010).

Preservation Office, Utah Division of State History. "Ogden's 'Grand Hotel'—the Bigelow—Preserves a Historic Area." *History Blazer* (September 1995).

Websites

"About Us." Rainbow Gardens. Accessed August 2016. http://rainbowgardens.com/rainbow-gardens-about.

"America's Fastest-Growing Cities 2016." *Forbes Business*, March 8, 2016. Accessed May 2016. http://www.forbes.com/sites/erincarlyle/2016/03/08/americas-fastest-growing-cities-2016/#2dfc06727056.

Anderson, Rebecca. "Intermountain Indian School." Utah Humanities, 2012. Accessed July 2016. http://www.utahhumanities.org/stories/items/show/4.

Armes, Deann. "Michael Fenton of Ogden's Ben Lomond Hotel." *City Weekly*, October 22, 2014. Accessed September 2016. http://www.cityweekly.net/utah/michael-fenton-of-ogdens-ben-lomond-hotel.

Billings, Molly. "The Influenza Pandemic of 1918." Stanford University, June 1997. Accessed April 2016. https://virus.stanford.edu/uda.

Bowsher, Kim. "A History of Violence: Ogden's 25th Street." Utah Stories, 2014. Accessed May 2016. http://utahstories.com/2014/08/a-history-of-violence-ogdens-25th-street.

Bradford, Kathleen. "Bushnell General Hospital." Utah Education Network. Accessed July 2016. http://www.uen.org/utah_history_encyclopedia/b/BUSHNELL_HOSPITAL.html.

Brown, Dylan. "Utah's Shooting Star Saloon Frozen in time." *Standard Examiner*, March 6, 2014. Accessed August 2016. http://www.standard.net/Local/2013/10/06/Utah-s-Shooting-Star-Saloon-frozen-in-time.

"Get Ye to an Abandoned Nunnery!" WeirdUS.com. Accessed August 2016. http://weirdus.com/states/utah/stories/abandoned_convent/index.php.

Hardy, Rodger. "Shhh…Do You Hear Someone Weeping?" *Deseret News*, October 18, 2005. Accessed August 2016. http://www.deseretnews.com/article/635154141/Shhh----Do-you-hear-someone-weeping.html.

Moore, Carrie. "Legends Surround St. Ann's Retreat." *Deseret News*, July 22, 2006. Accessed September 2016. http://www.deseretnews.com/article/640196655/Legends-surround-St-Anns-Retreat.html.

"Peery's Egyptian Theater." HauntedHouses.com. Accessed September 2016. http://www.hauntedhouses.com/states/ut/ogden-theater.htm.

Roberts, Richard. "Ogden." Utah History to Go. Accessed April 2016. http://historytogo.utah.gov/places/ogden.html.

Smith, Grant. "Main Theatre." Utah Theaters, June 28, 2004. Accessed August 2016. http://www.utahtheaters.info/TheaterMain.asp?ID=181.

Snyder, Brady. "Planner Hopes to Unearth Key Part of Ogden's Past." *Deseret News*, August 3, 2001. Accessed July 2016. http://www.deseretnews.com/article/856658/Planner-hopes-to-unearth-key-part-of-Ogdens-past.html.

Sullivan, Jack. "Fred Kiesel Opposed Church Rule in Utah and Prospered." Those Pre-Pro Whiskey Men!, August 24, 2014. Accessed May 2016. http://pre-prowhiskeymen.blogspot.com/2014/08/fred-kiesel-opposed-church-rule-in-utah.html.

Turney, Shawn, Nancy Van Valkenburg and Van Summerill. "Peery's Egyptian Theater." Cinema Treasures. Accessed September 2016. http://cinematreasures.org/theaters/238.

"Union Pacific Depot 800 West and Forest Street." Self-Guided Tours of Historic Sites. Brigham City, Utah. Accessed September, 2016. http://brighamcity.utah.gov/self-guided-tour-of-historic-sites.htm.

Van Leer, Twila. "Flu Epidemic Hit Utah Hard in 1918, 1919." *Deseret News*, March 28, 1995. Accessed April 2016. http://www.deseretnews.com/article/412123/FLU-EPIDEMIC-HIT-UTAH-HARD-IN-1918-1919.html.

Waite, Thorton. "Union Pacific Depots in Utah." Utah Rails, March 29, 2011. Accessed May 2016. http://utahrails.net/up/brigham-city-depot.php.

Newspapers

Goodwin's Weekly, October 12, 1918.

Logan Republican, August 9, 1917.

Los Angeles Times, January 12, 1950.

Ogden Standard, January 26, 1909; May 7, 1913; April 25, 1897; April 29, 1897; September 7, 1906; October 8, 1914; August 4, 1910.

Ogden Standard-Examiner, October 6, 1905; March 4, 1922; March 15, 1923; March 16, 1923; February 26, 1923; July 18, 1923; November 22, 1924; May 30, 1938; October 11, 1945; July 7, 1942; August 4, 1949; March 20, 1929.

Salt Lake Herald, April 30, 1897.

Salt Lake Tribune, April 25, 1897; August 7, 1907; November 8, 1942; October 17, 1943; April 5, 1946.

Springville Herald, January 26, 1939.

Interviews

Anonymous. 2016. Interview with owner of Shooting Star Saloon by author. September 14.

Anonymous. 2016. Interview with previous owner of Crystal Hot Springs by author. September 28.

Other

Utah Death Certificate Index, 1905–1965. Series 20842. Utah Department of Administrative Services. Division of Archives & Records Service.

ABOUT THE AUTHOR

After a lifelong fascination with the paranormal, Jennifer Jones decided to actively investigate the paranormal for herself and founded a very successful and busy paranormal team in 2007. She spent the next six years actively investigating haunted locations throughout Utah and other locations across the United States. While pursuing a degree in history, she realized that there was one major thing lacking from most paranormal investigations: in-depth, accurate research into the history of the locations and the people associated with them. While she still enjoys the occasional paranormal investigation, she has spent the last few years focusing on her blog, *The Dead History*, bringing to life the true history of haunted locations across the United States using historical records and facts. When she is not researching or writing about the paranormal, she enjoys spending time with her family, traveling and picking up new creepy objects to add to her collection.